ISSUE #120, WINTER 2020

ST. JOHN, KANSAS

CHIRON review
Issue #120, WINTER 2020

Poetry Editors
Wendy Rainey, Clint Margrave
Kareem Tayyar, Grant Hier

Fiction Editors
Rafael Zepeda, Sarah Daugherty

Art /Design: Craig Ashby

Cover photo: Andre Estevez

Chiron Review is indexed by *Humanities International Complete*. Issues 18-81 were indexed by *Index of American Periodical of Verse*. CR is microfilmed by ProQuest, Ann Arbor, MI, and its archive is housed at Beinecke Rare Book & Manuscript Library, Yale U., New Haven, CT.

Opinions expressed by the writers and artists in this journal are their own and not to be considered those of the publisher or the editors.

ISSN: 1046-8897

ISBN: 9781716337390

Copyright © 2020. All rights reserved under International and Pan-American copyright conventions. No part of this review may be reproduced, stored in a retrieval system, or transmitted in any form, electronic, mechanical, or other means, now known or hereafter invented, without written permission. Copyrights to all materials revert to the respective creator after publication.

Michael Hathaway, Publisher
chironreview2@gmail.com / www.chironreview.com

Donations are welcome via PayPal with this email address, editor@chironreview.com, check, or money order.

to the memory of
Lyn Lifshin
(1942-2019)

Contents

Joan E. Bauer / 7

Brenton Booth / 26

Adam Church / 45

Joan Colby / 39

Sandy Coomer / 46

Rachel Custer / 35

Michael Czyzniejewski / 30

Sarah Daugherty / 78

W.D. Ehrhart / 47

Edward Field / 14

Marja Hagborg / 65

Ruth Moon Kempher / 67

Kyle Laws / 71

Lyn Lifshin / 74

klipschutz / 78

Paul Lindholdt / 134

Anthony Lucero / 77

Ron McFarland / 95, 134

Tamara Madison / 92

DS Maolalai / 89

Alicia Mathias / 90

Fox Mederos / 49

Roger Netzer / 15

Gerald Nicosia / 132

Chika Onyenezi / 96

Jonah Raskin / 132

James Reed / 102

Diane Sahms / 109

Steve Sibra / 111

Kareem Tayyar / 115

David J. Thompson / 113

Jeri Thompson / 112

Charles Harper Webb / 130

Kristin Withers / 127

John Sibley Williams / 128

All But Lost

in the small print of NASA history
the story of my father: H.E. Bauer,
known as Hal, technical director

of that workhorse, the Saturn IV-B.
He's quoted on domes, propulsion,
structural integrity, welding

of the bulkhead. He's not quoted
on misanthropic pigeons, cost overruns,
entertaining "the brass" or how some rockets

blew to smithereens. His staff called him
"Dr. Bauer" though he only had four years
at LACC. In an audio recording,

he says: "Let me be specific."
His slow, deliberate voice sounds tired.
Missing from the records, his decades

in the Mojave, at Kwajalein, Holloman
& Huntsville, then Bremen for the Space Lab.
Unrecorded: the drag weight of being

"no-margin-for-error" responsible.
The struggle to de-pressurize. He had
that other family. Complications.

He's buried somewhere in Orange County.
I don't know where. I do have
a beer mug kind of trophy:

Eagle Has Landed
First Manned Lunar Landing
July 20, 1969
Hal Bauer A3 Mission Control

You can come over & see it anytime.

Joan E. Bauer

Labor Day

I'm driving to Sewickley on Route 65
where, distracted, speeding, I scored
three tickets the year my husband died.

Two polished stones in my back pocket.
Water & towels for the granite.
A notebook. Maybe something to record.

Tree-lined Sewickley, much the same.
Talbots, Penguin Books, the Antiquarian Shop.
Berkshire Hathaway, even Sotheby's.

For the holiday, a flurry of American flags.
Impatiens blossom in baskets on the lamp posts.
A "Doggy Bakery." That's new.

The cemetery is just above "The Village"
on a wooded hillside. The road is winding
& narrow. I go slow, uncertain of my bearings.
In fact, I'm lost.

Isn't he on the right there? Near a crossroad?
Did I miss a turn? Protestants, Catholics.
My husband, one of the only Jews.
There's a monument to the Tuskegee Airmen
that wasn't here before.

After some circling, I find him.
I sweep away some ants & a musky web.
The birth date is wrong. Somehow, I gave him
an extra year.

Over the ridge, some rain is coming.
I loved him. For months, I was distraught,
but now, honestly, no words.

I leave behind the stones, head home,
blasting through a yellow
to beat the storm.

Joan E. Bauer

Gray Wolf

*It was in the Dark Time, after the Collapse
of the Spiraling Suns –*

Alone in the forest, Gray Wolf had lived
a hundred years. He was not like the others.
He roamed but returned each night

to the dark grove where Owl Tree stood
scorched by a forgotten fire. Some nights
Gray Wolf gazed through Owl Tree's

empty eyes at the blighted moon.
Some days Gray Wolf thought –
Perhaps I'm not a wolf at all.

Owl Tree whispered:
Once you were a man. This day
you are wolf. Perhaps again a man.

~

Gray Wolf could not down a moose
or bear. Even when he caught their scent,
he couldn't. One day, he came upon

a wounded Girl near a fallen oak. He nosed
her blood-stained rags, almost tasting
her limbs. Something held him back.

He dragged her to a cave where she slept
for days. He washed her wounds, broke
a branch from Healing Tree & thought –

If this Two-Leg girl wakens, she will fear me.
When she woke, she touched his bristly fur
& thought: I must be dreaming.

He brought a branch of berries,
spread them before her. She spoke:
You are a wolf, yet I do not fear you

not thinking Gray Wolf would answer.
But with gentle moan & bark, he did.
Somehow she knew his meaning.

They sought out Owl Tree who warned:
You're not who you believe.
You must find a deeper forest.

~

The Girl & Gray Wolf lived in peace
until the coyotes found him. A creature
possessed, she rushed to save him,

thrashing at the coyotes with thorn bushes.
She made a sled to bear him back, took leaves
from Healing Tree to salve his wounds.

But maggots appeared. Surely he was dying.
Blind rage overwhelmed her. She left him
behind to search for a smoking stick.

She knew its use & found one. Then a voice:
That is not the way – She returned to find
the maggots feasting on his wounds.

At first she pulled them away, but remembered:
She'd heard it said that maggots help with healing.
So she fed him a broth of fruit & herbs.

In time, they returned to Owl Eyes
pleading: Make us Two-Legs, or Four,
so that we may live together.

Owl Eyes stood silent. Then a piercing cry.
A sudden wind & storm engulfed them.
Lightning split an ancient oak. Nearby

the howl of coyotes, but when the winds
subsided, only a shimmer of dust,
rain-soaked earth & scattered leaves.

Joan E. Bauer

Roger Netzer

An Interview with Edward Field

ROGER NETZER: When people say they like Edward Field, they don't just mean they like his poems. They mean they like the person whom they encounter, or imagine they encounter, in the poems. Why do you think it is that readers like *you*, not just your poems?

EDWARD FIELD: Readers know you don't have to be formal with me. So you can just be yourself. You can relax.

You want the poet's voice to be someone you feel comfortable with and who communicates – not too self-involved or private.

ROGER: A poet is a man speaking to men?

EDWARD: Just speaking to your people. It's sort of like a public role, speaking to your people, but at the same time you're being one of them.

ROGER: The title of your first book, *Stand Up, Friend, With Me,* offers friendship.

FIELD: The use of the word friend is solidarity as much as friendship. With me it was a call to political action, vaguely.

Richard Howard interpreted it in the Freudian sense: The little friend is a man's little friend, his penis. But I saw it in the Marxian sense in which you're saying workers of the world unite. Stand up and throw off you chains.

ROGER: Solidarity with your penis is another strain in your poems.

EDWARD: It's man's best friend.
ROGER: Did the poets whom you admired offer solidarity?
EDWARD: Auden did, and of course I immediately latched on to Auden. My poetry got less formal as it went along until finally there was Cavafy who was totally intimate and friendly.

Back when I started writing, poetry was divided into two branches: light verse, which was anything that was funny; and then serious poetry. You could never have a joke in serious poetry. Auden bridged the gap, which was so liberating because before Auden, light verse was humorous but not serious and not profound.

But of course Jews look at it differently and the humor in Jewish tradition was wisdom. I've often thought that the Book of Job could be translated funny.

ROGER: How long after you started writing poetry were you able to be funny in verse?

EDWARD: I didn't know a lot of it was funny. I only learned that when I read it in public and people laughed.

ROGER: What was it like to hear the laughter?

FIELD: I loved it. It was a revelation. I mean for people to laugh at a poetry reading wasn't very common. It may be more common now.

ROGER: Once at a reading, you moved the lectern aside and said, 'I think you're entitled to the whole poet.'

EDWARD: To say, 'I'm not just a head, I'm below the waist, too.' Words come out of the body. They don't come out of the head only. You feel the words coming out of the body when you think of them. They're part of your physical being.

ROGER: You are referring to the moment of composing the poems as well.

EDWARD: If they're true, they'll always feel like they're part of the body. They're physical.

If they come to you in the head ... but that's not where they come from. I mean you can tell it's poetry not prose by where they come from. Because the prose is from a different center – rom somewhere else.

ROGER: In 'A Full Heart' you wrote:

The great leap
over the gap
between thinking of an idea
and writing it down.

When you first write something down that might be a poem, how much of it resembles the final poem?

EDWARD: Occasionally a whole poem comes out, but mostly it's an idea and then the poem is implicit and it's buried in those first words. But the exact words – well I always meant what I said, the gap between thinking of something and writing it down is that you have to get the exact words. So it has to be put down immediately because two minutes later the words change.
You're going to just change a word or two and that will make all the difference. It's very hard to get the exact words down so you have to get them right down.

It's a question of whether you have the nerve to go on. I'm not writing much down at the moment. I mean I'm writing down a lot of beginning poems. I think I could actually get back to them when I'm ready to write.

ROGER: Are there poems that you finish years after beginning them?

EDWARD: I love having a poem on my computer screen as I work. Just such fun to have! Especially if I'm in a fairly dry period then it's wonderful to work on tough technical problem in poetry. Because poetry isn't actually easy, it's very ... it's got a very structured language, so you have to always keep juggling it. Finding, turning around. I love it when I can turn whole stanzas around and make a first line out of a last line.

ROGER: You prefer word-processing to typing?

EDWARD: It's so much easier. You can block and move on the screen. You can move a whole section to somewhere else. Endlessly. I love doing that. The one problem is: You don't have a record of all your worksheets.

ROGER: You can always 'open in a new version.'

EDWARD: I never do that. I cannot do that. I just have to keep changing the one draft on screen. You can't go back to early versions. What it is, is what it develops to be.

ROGER: Do your poems go through a great deal of revision?

EDWARD: Yes, because I learned to write poetry during the new criticism when everybody bragged about how many drafts they did. It was really Yeats who started all of that. When Yeats got his monkey balls installed, his writing changed tremendously. His poem 'Byzantium' and others like it, that was an entirely different tone than his previous lyrical poetry. This was hard work, this poetry.

ROGER: If we had in front of us an early draft of a poem by you and the final version, how different would they look?

EDWARD: Well I can't say. I never compare ...

ROGER: Is revision for you a process of making it clearer and clearer and clearer?

EDWARD: Somebody once said poetry should be at least as good as prose. But in reworking and revising I'm always trying to put in what is missing. Revising is not only to correct what's not said right, or because you didn't get the words down right, or to take out what's unnecessary. You have to put in what's missing. That takes time.

It's really nice to look at a poem day after day. I don't see how people can do it all at once, but then there are people for whom it's easier than me.

I'm not really a very verbal person. I don't have an easy way with words. Maybe because I come from an immigrant family that didn't speak very good English.

ROGER: The tone and rhythm of Edward Field's everyday speech has much in common with his poetry. But you are not a person who dominates conversation the way your friend Frank O'Hara did.

EDWARD: But my poems are getting longer. They're more talkative. So if they want to talk ...

ROGER: Your poetry is conversational?

EDWARD: I don't want to scare anybody away. If you say I'm going to read a poem, everybody freezes and then of course they're surprised when it's almost like somebody talking to them. They can hear it and the words – it's not scary.

ROGER: Although you can be very clear and very easy and still be scary.

EDWARD: A lot of this hasn't occurred to me because I don't bother with it. I just do it. Well, I used to.

There's some place in the body that creates the words of poetry. It's not prose, and I'm feeling my midsection. It's a place in there where tears are and also nausea and let's see what else is in there?

ROGER: Your solar plexus?

EDWARD: Yes, but then tears are there. Everything is there and the poetry sort of goes through there. I don't know if it comes from there.

ROGER: Was there a time you became concerned about how intimate tour poems can be?

EDWARD: You mean unpublishable?

ROGER: Is that how you think of it?

EDWARD: That's where the problem was. There are certain requirements of publishing and one is you can't say certain things.

ROGER: Did you feel an affinity with the confessional poets? They published intimate and personal poems.

EDWARD: Robert Lowell supposedly started confessional poetry. When he talked about hitting his father it was sort of disgusting. He objected to something his father said – sort of, how dare you say this to me, your son? We have a formal relationship and so I knock you down like a man would a gentleman. Give me a break. No, he never was confessional. Not by my standards.

ROGER: Frank O'Hara was someone who presented an attractive persona in his poetry.

EDWARD: His words were him. He spoke that way. He didn't have to do anything except write it down because that was him in words. It always seemed very easy to me the way he wrote, but then he was the kind of person that didn't have to revise. He was so developed he'd never say anything crude or, I don't know, clumsy. He was always an elegant gentleman. So his poetry is that way. He was always way ahead of me who had to struggle to get to the poems.

ROGER: You do not shy from political engagement in your poems.

EDWARD: That is the Jewish tradition, which I'm very much a part of. Even the Biblical tradition. I'm not going to get up there and preach to the masses but I denounce seeing all this stuff. Well the prophets actually denounce the rulers more than the people. But then also there's the Jewish folk tradition of Jewish socialism which I grew up with.

ROGER: What's that tradition?

EDWARD: Eastern European Jews are all socialists.

ROGER: So you grew up with it in sense of reading it or just hearing it expressed?

EDWARD: Just having it in my fold because it was part of the tradition of my parents, too. My mother did talk about it sometimes, she was more political than my father. But it just creeps in and poetry has to say something to people.

It's a socially responsible attitude. That is part of it. I think Jewish poets from the sweatshop, sweatshop poets, they did talk to the lowliest people. The poorest people were their audience and they all were socialists and talked about what was possible. Mankind making a better world for itself.

ROGER: Are poets the unacknowledged legislators of mankind?

EDWARD: No, but I think I say in a poem I could solve the problems of the world if they asked me.

ROGER: Your verse welcomes not just the individual reader but many kinds of readers, too. From the inception of your career the poems respect and even cherish what we now call diversity.

EDWARD: Yes, the thing is we are all human beings. Whereas a lot of poets say, 'I'm exclusive,' 'I'm superior.' I mean there's a whole thing in the literary world of 'I'm superior.'

And that's one thing New York excels in. I tried, in doing my anthology *A Geography of Poets*, to show that all around the country there are people who are writing it.

ROGER: You decided to become a poet when you were already an adult man.

EDWARD: When I really seriously started to write was in 1948, when I went to Paris to be a poet.

ROGER: When was your first poem published?

EDWARD: Then. I was sending out my poems immediately.

ROGER: So as soon as you started sending them, you started getting accepted.

EDWARD: A lot of rejections and a few acceptances, yes. Once I started really writing, then I got published because it was already poetry.

ROGER: What was your first poem that was published?

EDWARD: A rhymed poem in quatrains. I was in love with this Swedish tourist. A bunch of Swedes came to this little fishing village I was spending the summer, and his name was Sigvard. And I said goodbye to him on the train and it was very emotional.

ROGER: This was not unrequited love?

EDWARD: Not quite unrequited. *Just* requited. He gave me a picture of himself with a heart split in two in the back. I thought that was pretty good. It didn't need to be consummated. It was returned but not consummated, whatever that is.

ROGER: We can't find these early poems of yours. They're not in your books.

EDWARD: Actually someone just found the magazine and gave it to me.

ROGER: Let the record reflect the poet has stood and is walking through the ivory halls of his home to his stately archive.

EDWARD: [laughing] This is my second publication, in *Botteghe Oscure*, published in Rome by the American heiress Princess Marguerite Caetani. There was a department store on Union Square that she owned. And she used the proceeds to pay for this magazine. It was edited by T.S. Eliot actually. Here it is:

> Ice on the bone shivered me south
> To a dream of figs and sun-filled days;
> A fortress crumbles at the harbor mouth
> And fishermen loaf on the quais.
> Old, bent, and black-robed women mend
> Burnt-umber nets upon the sand,
> And rows of pastel houses bend
> on the harbor like a hand.
> But bursting the purple days, the swords
> Of Vikings took the town for prize;
> In olive groves yawned rock-bound fjords
> And the fortress sang to blue eyes.
> Hot on the arc of sand beats the sun,
> But my slow blood races to their chill seas
> As I stand on the southern quais alone
> In the nets of a northern breeze.

Now that is actually my first successful poem.

ROGER: Which of the poems in your books was the earliest written?

EDWARD: The first poem in *Stand Up, Friend, With Me*.

ROGER: 'Prologue.' From the group subtitled 'Greece.'

EDWARD: I wrote those poems in Greece when I was living there in 1949.

ROGER: So some of the poems from you first book, which was published in 1963, were written 14 years earlier.

EDWARD: They reflect ... I had discovered Cavafy.

ROGER: So in fact you hit your mature style pretty fast once you started writing.

EDWARD: I guess so.

ROGER: When was it that people observed the distinctiveness of your voice?

EDWARD: I only think that when my first book was published then and it won a prize and then it was taken seriously.

ROGER: When did William Carlos Williams see your poems?

EDWARD: He saw my earlier manuscript. He praised me. But he was very generous.

ROGER: Not to everybody.

EDWARD: I don't know. [Laughter.] An editor actually had discovered me already. And he was hoping my poetry would develop further and it didn't. David McDowell at New Directions was going to put me into a book of three young poets, a series of three young poets. So you wouldn't have your own book. And then he showed the poems to William Carlos Williams who confirmed his opinion that I was talented. And then he never published me because he said it hadn't developed. I was having a hard time. I was having a very hard time living my life. And so, my writing was going in all directions.

ROGER: What do you mean going in all directions?

EDWARD: I came back from Paris in 1950 and I had nothing, no idea how to live my life. I had no degrees; I didn't want an academic life. I didn't want advertising or publishing or any of those things that poets did. The so-called sympathetic jobs you could get. I didn't want to do any of that, I said, so maybe I'd work in a factory. So I worked in a warehouse. To try to be a poet of the people, the idea was to get a job with other people and live the life like other people, because you can't be a poet if you do that.

And poetry was sort of limping along in the 50s and I met Frank O'Hara and he showed me well, just write what you can in the time you have and with what comes and just accept that. And I have accepted that attitude.

ROGER: You speak modestly about the poem being friendly, of not scaring people away. But then there is that other poetic desire: to amaze with verbal dexterity and spiritual magic. To be prophetic, speaking words that are the most powerful that can be spoken.

EDWARD: Yeah.

ROGER: Surely you must, at times, experience pride and power in what you do and have done?

EDWARD: Yes, I do. And, in fact, it's made my old age pretty satisfying. It's very nice to have done what I've done. I was thinking the other day that I really have very few regrets. It's amazing how all of that Freudian stuff went away in my eighties, the conflicts and situations and all the psychological problems, almost all of them went away.

ROGER: But not before you made use of them?

EDWARD: Yes. They were material. Back when I started, poetry wasn't supposed to be therapy, and for me it always has been. My poem 'The Tailspin' ends with 'I can, I can ...' Okay, what's the last line?

ROGER: And that way come out of your tailspin whole.

EDWARD: In other words, I underline, I'm not sure I approve of that. I underline the message.

ROGER: That particular poem heals people. They read that poem and it changes their life.

EDWARD: Oh. Wow.

ROGER: You were not aware of that?

EDWARD: You can't go on writing if you think about those things.

ROGER: 'The Tailspin' is cleverly crafted.

EDWARD: Yeah, well it carries its metaphor through quite competently.

ROGER: Just as in a more recent poem, your airplane metaphor got carried through in 'Cataract.'

EDWARD: Exactly.

ROGER: While your poems can look like they are just going naked, in fact they are always quite elegant too.

EDWARD: If you can get the exact words for something it gets generally elegant and those often have to come – to begin with they come and then the work begins – you have to write the rest of the poem.

ROGER: So, what comes first? Words, or just the concept?

EDWARD: No. A few wonderful words.

ROGER: And do those few wonderful words remain your favorite lines in the poem or sometimes do you suddenly discover something else, a piece of the puzzle that just falls in?

EDWARD: I think one of my ideals is Stephen Spender's 'I think continually of those who are truly great,' which ends: 'And left the vivid air signed with their honour.' [Laughter]. My favorite last line in poetry.

But poems don't have to end dramatically or that elegantly. They can just end.

ROGER: When is a poem finished?

EDWARD: When you can't do anything more. It's not that you finish it, but that you can't do anything more with it. And then enough of it is there and hopefully nobody but you will see the flaws. I have changed poems that have been published.

ROGER: Like W.H. Auden.

EDWARD: Not big changes, like his 'September 1, 1939.' Nothing that extreme, but I have changed some words here and there. In my poem 'World War II,' I tried to add in that the tail gunner was gay. I put it in and now I've taken it out again.

ROGER: That poem is doing so much already.

EDWARD: I know, but I thought, well I ought to let people know there were gay people in the war.

I read some lines from 'World War II' for a German documentary recently. Just the opening because it talks about flying into the flak. The whole idea of the documentary is about the anti-aircraft gunners in World War II. So I represented what they were shooting at and how it felt to fly into the field of exploding shells and flying right through. They kept trying to make me say I was afraid and I kept saying, no it's something called displacement: Fear turns to excitement.

ROGER: And, you're working.
EDWARD: And you're working. And so, of course, they had a hard time accepting.
ROGER: That poem is like an action movie. Literally:

You black out, and then come to
with water rushing in like a sinking ship movie.

EDWARD: I discovered that what can hold a poem together is the narrative. And you can do it various ways. Once you give up rhyme and meter and verses and stanzas, then the poem has to hold it together by itself.

You can do it various ways. It can be a syllogism. Prayers hold together – the 23rd Psalm, which is the great healing poem. So I just discovered that if you could tell a story it could be a narrative structure to the poem.

ROGER: But you don't give up the line breaks. How do you figure out line breaks?

EDWARD: I know you're supposed to know why you do things but I just do it by instinct. What sounds like a good line? Sometimes I've experimented making the lines shorter and breaking the phrases up. I try not to break up phrases except for drama, for emphasis, something like that.

It should be an indication of how to read it. You're giving instructions to the reader. That's why poetry is clearer than prose. Because prose is just written on the page in blocks. That's why I can't really understand anybody bothering with a prose poem because the wonderful thing about poetry is that it does tell you how to read it. Your blocks, your lines, are a sequence of the developing ideas. So it's really quite useful.

ROGER: Do you have a favorite among the photographs of you on your books?

EDWARD: No. I don't really like them much. I'm not sure.

ROGER: You don't like photographs of yourself generally?

EDWARD: I don't like my looks particularly. I mean, I was always a thin, ugly, dark Jewish boy in school with curly hair. You were supposed to have straight hair and light eyes and pale skin and ...

ROGER: Whose looks would you like to have?
EDWARD: Oh well, when you put it that way I realize I don't want to be anyone else. I like the difficult, it's difficult being me, but it's ok. I like the task.

* * *

Minor Accident of War

a new short film by Diane Fredel-Weis
based on a poem by Edward Field

This new animated film is more than 70 years in the making.

A team of award-winning filmmakers created this unique film inspired by a veteran's harrowing experience as navigator, flying in the largest air raid over Berlin in World War II.

Since Edward Field survived that fateful night in 1945, to authoring the poem in 1967, to recording the narration for the film on his 95th birthday this year, *Minor Accident of War* transcends time and place with raw emotion and humanity.

Edward's niece, media producer Diane Fredel-Weis, has gathered a team of world-class artists, including animator Piotr Kabat, sound designer Michal Fojcik, composer Alex Gimeno, animation consultant Alex Kupershmidt, and co-producer David Finch, to create a truly unique film that combines history with contemporary artistry.

A Different View

The nut ward had
no windows,
only a small
outdoor area
with high walls
that gave a
view of the
sky if you tilted
your head the
right way.
It was winter
and cold
and I only had
shorts and a
t-shirt.
But I sat there
shivering on a
broken plastic
chair.
Liza sat on the
rubber floor
with her legs
crossed looking
at a painting of
sunflowers that
had been taped
to the wall.
We stayed there
for hours;
me seeing sky,
her seeing
sunflowers,
while the others
went crazy

inside,
and we hoped:
they'd
forget
us.

Brenton Booth

Factory

There's
an old
abandoned
building
I pass
every day
on my
way to
work.
The walls
are
crumbling
and roof
gave way
long ago
to all the
birds.
It is
surrounded
by a
barbed
wire fence
(to keep
out the
homeless)
and new
apartment
buildings.
My father
gave up
the best
years of
his life
to this
building.
Sewing
quality

leather
goods
under
harsh
false
light.
He went
from
athlete to
drunk to
drunken
husband:
with never
enough
money to
handle any
of it.
I often
think about
the old
building
standing
there after
all these
years,
working as
my father
once did;
in a
building
that will
one day
crumble:
but never
disappear.

Brenton Booth

Michael Czyzniejewski

Stick

Kids in stick prison own exactly one personal item: a stick. They can do whatever they want with the stick: peel the bark off, break it into pieces, whittle it, carve it, even burn it (though they have no access to knives or matches). They get one stick. It's their stick. They don't get another, no matter what happens to it, no matter how many years they're in stick prison. One stick per kid: That's the rule.

~

Kid are allowed to play with their personal sticks in their quarters most of the day. They are not allowed other toys, and aside from meals and the weekly communal hosing, they do not interact with the other inmates.

One game that remains popular is called "retrieve the stick." This is when a kid throws his or her stick across his or her quarters. When the stick has settled, the kid moves to recover the stick. Once the stick has been recovered, the kid has won that round of retrieve the stick. Best of all, the kid can repeat this game, again and again, as many times as he or she likes.

Since the quarters are not much larger than the kids themselves, retrieve the stick isn't all that challenging, the kid often needing to simply bend over or reach across him or herself to fetch the thrown stick. This accessibility makes retrieve the stick popular for new kids and long-term inmates alike.

~

Part of kid's routine in stick prison is dedicated to daily lessons: history, science, and math.

During history, kids learn the origin of their personal sticks, such as who the stick belonged to before it belonged to him or her and what famed lumberjack harvested the stick for the prison's use.

In science, kids learn about what type of tree their stick came from, under which climate that tree prospers, and what care, hypothetically, a living tree of their stick-kind would require.

In math, there is only one number: 1.

Kids in stick prison do not learn how to read or write, though years ago, some kids, using their sticks in a pen-like manner, were known to ape the stick prison guards making out their reports. This behavior is discouraged now, however, as it's been hypothesized that a kid, mimicking a guard long enough, could learn to write by accident. Today, a kid caught performing any type of writing simulation loses his or her stick for one week – no kid has ever faced such a penalty more than once, rest assured.

~

It is crucial kids get to know their own stick. They need to be able to identify it, no matter what. For example, as the kids enter the cafeteria, they all place their sticks in the stick box sitting just outside the door, as personal sticks are not allowed inside the cafeteria; this is so they're not confused with meal sticks, the sticks kids eat once a day. After the kids drop off their personal sticks in the stick box, they enter the cafeteria, grab a plate, and are served their meal stick by the kid working kitchen detail that day. They then sit down at their assigned seats and enjoy their meal stick. After, they pick their personal stick out of the stick box in the hallway and return to their quarters. Nearly a hundred kids eat during each meal period, so each kid leaving the cafeteria has to be able pick out his or her stick and rejoin the line, all without breaking stride. Kids, the first few weeks, often find this challenging, sometimes ending up with the wrong stick, even no stick at all. When a kid loses his or her stick, he or she has to live without a stick from there on out. These kids are branded as outliers, freaks, the kids without a stick. They have nothing to play with and nothing to talk to. It's a wake-up call for the whole facility: No one loses a stick for months, sometimes years, after some new kid loses his or her stick in the stick box at meal time.

~

    There are days designed to break the monotony of stick prison. The kids figure out it's Christmas when their meal stick is served in a bowl with water and sawdust, what the cafeteria matron refers to as "stick pudding."

    On the summer solstice, kids are allowed into the courtyard for exactly one hour to revel in the sunlight, breathe outside air, and collect dirt they can smear on their personal stick, mainly for decorative purposes. Traditionally, the children become horribly sunburnt during this hour, bringing the practices of the prison under criticism. One year, the local ACLU chapter sent a case of sunscreen prior to the solstice. It was distributed to the kids, most of whom promptly squeezed it into their mouths, consuming it. During their solstice hour, they all got sunburn, "... but only on the outside," the warden joked to the press. Sunscreen was never donated again.

    On each kid's birthday, he or she is allowed to open one piece of incoming mail. A few children have boxes and boxes of letters and parcels to choose from, though most kids don't have anything, their loved ones abandoning them. Those with options learn quickly not to choose anything that might have food inside, as all foodstuff is quickly confiscated and eaten by the guards as the kid watches. The popular choice is any thick, letter-sized envelope, the one that might hold the longest letter, the one with the most words. The kid is then allowed to read that letter over the course of their birthday, in their quarters, as many times as they want. Because most kids in stick prison have never learned to read, this has puzzled outsiders, including scholars. Several prominent psychologists have suggested "it's the thought that counts" for these children, that they believe a long letter implies a higher rate of affection from the writer – even if the long letter is a detailed explanation of the opposite. And it often is. The day after the kid's birthday, the letter is re-confiscated and burned, though the kid can request the letter's ashes, used mainly to smear on his or her stick, though some kids have been known to consume those as well.

~

Despite the instincts of many of the inmates, the kids are discouraged from naming their stick. In fact, naming a stick can add years, even decades, on to a kid's stick prison sentence. Early in the history of stick incarceration, kids were not only encouraged to name their stick, but to treat their stick like a living, breathing organism. Kid and stick coexisted, and over the course of the kid's detainment, they developed a special bond with their stick … a bond that troubled some very influential people. Before long, the practice of naming sticks – let alone forming a relationship – was banned. Any kid caught naming his or her stick would automatically lose that stick, and for good. With such a severe penalty, it's no surprise there's never been a need in the history of the stick prison system for this to happen.

Outsiders have suggested that many kids, despite the heavy price, venture to name their stick inside their own heads, perhaps whisper the stick its name in the dark of their quarters. Whether this is true or not, no one can say. But we like to think the kids in our stick prison are good kids, embracing their rehabilitation. The naming of a stick would violate that belief, the trust between system and variable. Therefore …

Kids do not name their sticks.
They do not talk to them.
They certainly do not love them.
And their sticks do not love them back.

~

"Are you really sending us to stick prison?" my kids want to know.

"After dinner," I tell them. "Maybe even before."

"What if we're really good from now on?"

"We'll have to see," I say. "But you were pretty bad."

The oldest, my daughter, looks skeptical. She's just turned 6. I tell her that girl from her kindergarten class, Amarisa – who moved to Chicago the previous month – didn't really move, but was sent to stick prison; she fought with her sister, didn't listen to her parents, and was generally bad. A look of terror flashes across her face. I can see her imagining sweet little Amarisa, holding her stick, shivering in a dark cell.

My youngest, almost three, begins to cry. He says he doesn't want to go to stick prison, that he'll be good. Swears it. Apologizes over and over for hitting his sister. Says he'll never do it again as long as he lives. We pull up to the house. I ask him to stop, tell him it'll be okay, but he runs inside, bawling. My daughter follows. By the time I gather all the groceries and am standing in the kitchen, they have found my wife, each of them clenching one of her legs. They are red and exasperated and howling. My wife appears furious.

"They wouldn't stop fighting. Cameron hit Belinda in the face and Belinda hit him back, right in the eye."

"So you threatened them?"

The household is quiet the rest of the evening.

For dinner, I make a stir fry. Before we sit down, I go to the yard and fetch a stick from the birch next to the deck. There are countless sticks lying about, hundreds, making it impossible to keep up. I leave them there, on the deck, where they mock me.

When my wife and the kids come to the table, they have rice and chicken and vegetables on their plates and I have the birch stick. The kids look wide-eyed, then laugh. My wife comes around when I pretend to cut the stick with my fork and knife. I apologize to the kids for scaring them and they apologize for how they behaved. I put the stick aside and reach for the rice, but my wife slaps my hand. She nods down at the stick. The kids glare at it, too. I fork it back on my plate. We say grace. Then I go to it, first a nibble, the tiniest bit of bark. Next I take a bite, gnawing through the brittle edge, gnashing into the wood. The pieces never really get smaller as I chew, so they go down whole. I abandon chewing, big, pointy pieces cutting their way through my throat. I know I'm lucky, though, when I spy a glass of milk off to the side, a creamy stick milkshake in my near future.

First Communion

Outside the sanctuary, a little girl,
        Eyes hooded beneath her hands, like throats
Widening dark around a song. Inside

        The sanctuary, a desperate man. How lonely
we are, locked inside yesterday.
        How like our fingers, always undoing

Buttons God done up, buttons we
        Had better left undone. Inside a holy robe,
A man might find his own trembling

        thighs, might with his hands undo
a little girl. A man might wrap his need around
        the open throat of her gaze,

might drop himself like prayer into the dark.

Rachel Custer

Mercy, Defined

Mercy was a girl grown
wise to the world's lies

winter whipping her back like a testament

to youth, that early fervor
no girl survives

Mercy shaved a pork bone
down to a fine point, used it

to pick the gristle from her teeth.

What is a world?
        Another set of hands pawing a girl.

What is a girl?
        A mouth like a sprung trap.

Rachel Custer

Written On the Edge of Sleep

Evening shuffles home, an invalid
        laboring under heavy bags of light

toward God, the distant, hopeful door
        of night. We know just enough of fear
to fear ourselves, to carry our weary

selves inside like drunks. Collapse inside
        the cells of other eyes. Arise! The day

comes soon enough to hope, dragging
        dawn behind it like a child. Toward
God, crouched down inside us, a rising

smile. Home is the dwelling place
        we make of hope. Hope the plodding
                pace we set toward home.

Rachel Custer

Mary the Mother of God Answers God the Father

I sing forever that which you call myth.

Throb beneath the skin of my wrists
myth. Pulse of my neck beneath a kiss
myth. This myth:

each tale a woman spins, spins her.

God, you grow inside me like an urge
and won't I name you? Won't I make your story
mine? Suckle you beneath my song alone.

I am dangerous in necessary ways –

the homeland his feet will always turn toward,
even when he lifts his face to you. My memory
like perfume filling his nose.

It takes a mother to birth
a God, a truth from myth. Father, that's all

you need to know.

Rachel Custer

Macular Degenerations

> *What should books teach*
> *But the art of living.*
>   – Samuel Johnson

When her central vision shrank
Into the black hole
Of all universal losses,
It was sudden
As the light that blinded Saul
On the road to Damascus.

He was converted, she was
Disillusioned. Years of prayer
And unquestioning faith dissolved
In the darkness where text
Blurred into the arguments
She'd shrugged off. Her husband,
The unbeliever. She made novenas
And buried him in sanctified dirt once
He had no say. She fought with the ophthalmologist
Who told her she'd be sorry – he was the best.
The laser did not help anyway.

Light lurked at the periphery
Like good intentions so she could grope
Her way through rooms remembering
The disposition of furniture. Her
Green eyes a slurry of all she missed.

She squinted at the photo of her
First grandchild, muttering bitterly,
"I can't see him."

The talking books she listened to
Implied one sense could replace another.

She sneered at platitudes like that. Books were
To entertain: the mysteries of Agatha Christie
Or Erle Stanley Gardner.

She sat by the TV. If she tilted her head
A certain way, she could glimpse a shade
Of movement that reminded her how, driving,
Sometimes a deer in roadside brush
Appeared, ready to lunge into her lane.
Just like sin, always waiting
In ambush for a woman
Who had lost her sight.

Joan Colby

Two Gifts

A straw devil mask given me
By the woman in Merida selling oranges
That are small and bitter.
I suck them dry.

A terracotta chacmool,
Cheap stuff for the busloads of tourists
Ascending the interior of the great pyramid
Where the original, enshrined with a ray of light,
Praises the Jaguar throne.

I walk beneath the colonnades
In the Temple of the Warrior.
A snake shakes its castanets
In the stony shadows.

These are the gifts
I choose to bring you:
A threat and an offering.

Turkeys stroll about the thatched huts.
Every night red snapper
And watermelon. I eat what is in season.
Bats fly over the cenotes
Beneath a suffering moon.

The coral reefs with
Brilliant little fish. An underworld
So beautiful, one could drown in it

Years later, the mask hangs
In the summer kitchen.
The chacmool perches on the pine desk.
Artifacts of some division
Half forgotten, gathering dust.

V-Mail

Fingering the keys of my daughter's Steinway,
I remember the tiny tissue-thin V-mails
From my cousin Pat. I was 5 years old.
He was 19. A sailor on The Franklin. He wrote
"Keep practicing your piano and one day
You'll play as well as Maxine." That was his fiancé.

I would be a flower girl in her wedding
When she married someone else. Pat's ship
Was sunk at Okinawa by a kamikaze plane.
I kept practicing with more determination
Than talent. I still have those yellowed v-mails
He'd printed carefully.

Joan Colby

November Blizzard

The plows have buried news
To disrupt a routine
Of coffee and pages.

In the background a voice speaks
Of outages and drifts.

We are lucky in light
And heat. The woodstove glows
The deep red of amnesty.

A snowflake rests on the feathers
Of a dark-eyed junco.

Boot prints punctuate the lane.
This is how far we can venture,
Our hearts drumming.

Remember Papa face-down in the snow
Still gripping the shovel.

How important is it to go
Into a world that murders
Expectations. That holds us hostage.

Frost patterns on the windows are ransom notes
That claim everyone will be freed.

Joan Colby

Enduring the Pain

Bone-deep, an ache of loss. Falling leaves renounce
Brilliance to cackle like brown hens. A footloose
Wretchedness. Fields of stubble stabbed with geese.
Pills, ointments, useless as a bible of fables,
Hearsay testimony as clouds of incense swing
From a golden thurible. Jays argue in the oaks.
Misery jabs its scalpel to twist sleeplessness
Into the dull novel you can't finish. Smoke of
Distant fires in the eucalyptus. Every door flinches
From the knock. The groan of persistent hinges.
Pain floats in dark oils, a citrus scent of hope
Comes and goes like someone scouting
Valuables. The ransom still unpaid.
Endure the scope, the brutal throb,
The delicacy of torment.

Joan Colby

Saint Cuddle

She is Saint Cuddle.
Diocese of babies
injected with addiction.

She descends and lifts
them out of the thorns.

Grasps their new bodies
and calms their shakes.

A prayer of peace:

I hope you find a
beautiful family.

I hope you get well
so you can play.

I hope you go to
college someday.

But study anything
other the liberal arts.

I hope you learn
perfect punctuation.

May your life after my arms
allow you to fly
higher than from where you came.

Adam Church

Flight

Juliane Koepcke, 17, was sucked out of an airplane after it was struck by lightning. She fell 2 miles to the ground still strapped to her chair and lived. She was the sole survivor of 93 passengers and crew in the crash of LANSA Flight 508 on December 24, 1971.

Can you
catch me? Hold
me to the spun insides
of a hot white light, a vortex
in brief windows, and then only
steel and wind. My breath strips sheer
as an angel's wing. I am an eagle with a
thousand talons aching for flesh, a hawk scanning
the seams of a broken earth. I am the sudden bullet that
drops the pheasant. I give a command and the hound howls
at the scent of blood. I am a flamingo, a blue heron, fish in the sky,
the memories from the reflection of grief. I am a red-winged blackbird,
a sparrow, a mockingbird repeating the mirrored sounds of the living. I live.
I curve through trees, and in that final rush of the dark, there's a holding, a stillness.

I curve through trees and there in the final rush of darkness, I hold the soft stillness
of sparrow, of mockingbird repeating the mirrored sounds of the living. I live
from the white memories of reflected grief. I am a red-winged blackbird
bearing the scent of blood. I am flamingo, blue heron, fish in the sky.
I am the pheasant dropped on command, and the hound howling
at the seams of a broken earth. I am the sudden bullet with
a thousand talons aching for flesh, a hawk scanning
for angels' wings. I am an eagle rising on
steel and wind. My breath strips sheer
the brief window and then only
light. A hot, white vortex
spins wildly inside me.
Catch me. Hold me
if you can.

Sandy Coomer

Celebrating the New Year

1968/1969

1.
We were bar-hopping in Hiroshima –
a strange and ghostly place,
nothing standing older than twenty-three years,
the whole city obliterated
by the first atomic attack,
scars on the hills around the city visible still.
Peace gas, Peace cigarettes, Peace candy bars:
white dove logos just about everywhere.
We'd been to the Peace Park already
where the only reinforced concrete structure
surviving the blast still stood,
a hollow, ghostly skeleton,
and the guestbook signed by visitors;
someone had written "Remember Pearl Harbor."
A fellow American, no doubt.

2.
But we were here tonight
to celebrate the New Year:
Fat Pat, Smitty, the Big Swede, and me.
God only knows what the locals thought of us,
but they liked our money
and we didn't make any trouble.
Somewhere along the way, we picked up
a bunch of young Norwegians,
merchant seamen, their freighter in port.
When the bars finally closed,
they invited us back to the *Arthur Stove*
and the party went on from there.
I remember beer, and a table loaded with food,
and a string of little paper Norwegian flags.
We somehow must have gotten some sleep,
but I don't remember when.

3.
I do remember stopping at Miyajima
on our way back to base the next day:
the Great Torii rising out of the bay,
the floating Shrine of Itsukushima,
the Five-storied Pagoda,
Sika deer by the hundreds,
gentle as house pets, unafraid.
And the women in all their New Year glory,
finest kimonos to start the year off right,
hiding their smiles behind their elaborate fans,
two little girls in kimonos, sisters perhaps,
so impossibly cute you wanted
to curl them up in your arms
and take them home to your Mom.

W.D. Ehrhart

Fox Mederos

Goat Story

On Pacer's monitor it was flesh tones. His computer glowed in orange, pink, and gold – a muted copulation, a virtual copy of the copy his client on the phones was watching. I was trying not to get caught looking. What I always do when I'm in one place for too long is get caught looking – and then Pacer looked up at me.

Across a purple line of DirecTV cubicles, only black squares of monitors bridged the gulf between us. This is porn time. It's understood and no one talks about it. I didn't have to say anything but when he saw me looking I said: "Porn calls, right?"

Pacer's brow furrowed. He had his hoodie up but now he was pulling it down. Pacer's hair was greasy black like an oil slick, same as the mustache on his top lip that he trimmed down into a goatee. His eyes were pinned to the dual screens in front of him. His knee jumped in checkered pajama pants stuffed into combat boots. I had only been on the DirecTV training program a week but decided to take special care not to attract specific types, veteran types who might want to commiserate, and this had been difficult because Klamath Falls didn't have many sorts of people that weren't veteran.

Everything about Pacer Everett was military. He tapped at the phone on his desk. "What's up, Raj? You need help?" he asked.

I waved, looking back to my monitor where my timesheet glowed a grim appraisal.

My Flex-Time burned in big red integers, a timekeeping system designed to ease the mental burden and low morale that came for television techs. The numbers on my screen reflected various many times that I had called out to go smoke in my car or drive fast in the one-lane highways. There would be no more PTO until I knuckled down, put in real time at the call-center, but the thought of more time in Klamath Falls, the glacial upper desert where pajamas to work was an acceptable mode of dress, made the liquid in my guts seize up. Still I wouldn't or couldn't close the Time Keeper. My mind arrested, I had not realized Pacer knew my name.

No calls came in for me while Pacer worked on his. Thirty minutes passed while I stared at a Showtime channel poster kit up for some David Duchovny comeback project. Duchovny in sunglasses with lights behind him, smirking at me while I, in the purple swivel chair, squeezed Silly Putty until it was a sooty shade of its original electric blue. I couldn't help but glance at Pacer.

"Okay try tuning to channel 621," he said. "Yeah, this is only a test channel. If your order is not playing on account of some dish misalignment then 621 should not play either." I tuned out of Pacer's porn call, this time with some grace. At the call center, I practiced non-thought now; instead of red-lining my four-cylinder four-door, I tried to be zen. To remove myself. Pacer cursed. He stood up from his desk, then he picked up the plastic of his phone receiver and slammed it. He was coming out of his headset, battering the keypad on his phone for a bathroom break. I was so close to going home that I could already feel my fingers freezing in my no-heater car.

"Hey, Raj Mahal," Pacer called to me.

"Yeah. Hold on," I said and dialed in a bathroom break.

"Say what you said to me again about porn calls."

His face lit up.

I told him: "All I said was, porn calls."

"Yeah? Well, you fucking said it, Pal. Look I'm not some holier-than-thou sort you sometimes find wandering these hallways but doesn't it feel like these motherfuckers should just be watching porn free off their phones like everyone else on the planet?"

I had little tricks for when someone made a joke. I would do one of those muted-laughs: first closing my eyes and then after bringing up my shoulders in one fluid motion – as if a fit of rolling booming thunder was going to break up and out of me but never would on account that I did not like to be seen laughing in public or for anyone to see the insides of my mouth. But Pacer seemed satisfied.

"You dialed out too, huh? Already twenty till. Fuck it right?" Pacer said.

"Did you fix it?"

Pacer reclined in his chair, suddenly set close to mine. "Yeah, I made him spin the satellite box around, tighten the SAT line and all that busy-work shit while I refreshed his feed from here. That did it just fine. I could hear the girls pumping on his set, carrying on: only filth on this cat's account – you wouldn't believe, Private. Then he tells me he can't control the volume on it. And then he says the channels don't change. Suddenly his remote don't work at all. So we run the script for remote: I check his batts, I switch between IR, to RF. We go through the television manufacturer codes yeah? I'm rattling numbers at him like NASA control trying to save Tom Hanks in space. And then he tells me: you know what he tells me?"

"Why'd you call me 'private'?" I said.

"He asks me if he needs the box spun around right-ways for his remote to work. He ain't spun it right since I made him tighten the SAT cable. I hung up on his ass. Fuck it."

"Did you know I served or something? Supervisor tell you? Who told you?"

"Everyone served out here." Pacer was smiling like a shark at me so that I recognized the smile and all the weird dirty jokes. "Say, I bet I look damn familiar to you now. Imagine me with a crew cut and no mustache."

Pacer's eyes had it; the rest of him had changed – gotten fat and grown hair in his nostrils, enough to disguise him. I badly wanted to leave but we were twenty-till and clocking out now would only sink my time lower. I had to knuckle down and put in real time. So I managed a casual confidence while my guts churned acid. "Oh shit, I do know you. That hurricane aid deployment down south. You and I set up at that flooded out little bank reserve right? I didn't know you lived up here."

"That's not all we did, is it? Now, I do some under the table private security down here at the Pink Elephant. Under the table pay I get is good, better than here. Do you know what I mean, Raj?"

"Pink Elephant, they do strippers and some slot machines right?"

But I was trying to push my memory back to the hurricane, a specific nagging concern that waved at me like a distant fog.

There was something wrong about Pacer I had learned the first time we'd met under all that rain in the flooded granite halls of a bank reserve but memories from that far back didn't come for me so well anymore. Because of all the non-thought. Because of the move and the stress and the Flex Time. Then I have it for a second, but it drops like a ring down a sink. The sound of a bell ringing.

"Still with me, Private?"

"Yeah what did you say?" I said.

"You remember I got court martialed. You ain't got to be polite – whole country heard about it."

"What was that again?" I said.

"That bank we were stationed at in the hurricane. That reserve building with the busted cage vault. If I walked away from it someone else woulda squeezed through right? So I grabbed it."

"Yeah, I remember we were there for a couple days. Watching Blackwater guys speed around on jet boats." When I said it, I could almost smell the septic water again. "You squeezed through the cage. Took a couple bullion."

"We," he said, after a long look around. Pacer's voice became a whisper I didn't like. "I only got court martialed because they never found all of it. Judge thought I kept some. I remember them tossing your shit, pulling out your bags. Not one lick of gold. How did you do it?"

"We?" I said.

"I ain't mad. But I think we can do better this time. So the Pink Elephant. They got hit by armed gunmen three times. They hired me to keep it quiet. They don't want people feeling like they can't gamble down there nor eat squaw sandwiches without someone driving an armored truck through the wall, amirite?"

"Someone drove a truck through the wall?" I said.

"Those sonsabitches ain't count on their truck getting jammed. It's still there if you wanna see. Construction crew has to build around them."

The small digital numerals clicked into formation and a prompt on my monitor came up reminding me to clock out to which Pacer replied, "Fuck it."

I clocked out. And I put the Silly Putty in a drawer that locked. And I put on my coat. All smooth in non-thought. For a while, I couldn't even smell Pacer's ripe-warm arm smell from his hoodie. I was in non-thought but Pacer was still talking about a safe.

"So Pink Elephant's got a safe. Ugly sonuvabitch with thick hinges and fat little legs that strain the carpet. Nearly blew my back out trying to help move it while they were renovating in there." Pacer sat back again. "What's that tell you? A place gets hit three times. Three different crews. Three different failed campaigns in search of the same prize yet the owner don't want to press charges. Hell you ever known white on red skin crime ever be forgotten much less forgiven in this country? What's that tell you?"

"I don't know. Desperate neighborhood. Klamath is drying up. You and I are sitting in her best paying job." I felt the blood draining from my arms to my feet, felt like I had been running with a pack on in the rain, felt like I had climbed a hundred stairs up out of Klamath Lake and now I was sitting back in it; it might as well have been a hole. That hole might as well have been flooding. Pacer went on, kicking the little flags I had labeled as triggers while he took us back. How could I have forgotten a whole person from my life?

When I looked up at Pacer, he was smiling. He put an arm around me, squeezed the back of my neck so that it hurt. "That's my point. You walked away and still ended up down here with me in Klamath Falls. Here we are again, another drowning city." Pacer's shoulders jumped with a laugh slick and slimy with insinuations. "You're in if you want it. I was going to talk to Fred who runs that airsoft bullshit every Halloween. But I'm talking to you."

II.

Pacer gave Sho a blue rubber prop-gun molded to look like a Glock nine-millimeter. While I loaded bullets into spare magazines for us, Pacer explained that it was Sho's job not to let this blue gun he called the 'Smurf' point at any human targets, his leg or anything by accident. If she got lazy and left it on her lap, pointed it at him or me, then she would have failed – she would be off the big heist, just like Fred. Pacer assured her that he and I both went through this training. I was never forced to do anything so humiliating in the Guard. When Sho looked at me I could see on her face that she knew it.

Sho and I were close but I barely recognized her when we picked her up at the trailer park on the east side of the lake. She was wearing yoga pants, and fake nails and had straightened out her hair for Pacer, I gathered. Sho was a Cree native; when she wasn't fixing porn playback at the call center, Sho danced at the Pink Elephant. Aside from me, she was the youngest at the call center training program, so we had hit it off quick. And Pacer knew. Sho would leave me salt water taffy on my desk every day at break, and I made it a point to kiss her grandma's cheek at the bank whenever I was running errands, even though I didn't like physical contact. I could tell Pacer didn't like our familiarity but I was puzzled about why he had brought her.

We drove into the woods a long time, then Pacer parked at the edge of a dried riverbed the size of a Malibu swimming pool. It was littered in beer cans and shell casings but everything else was wind and different variations of green. I imagined nothingness, for a hundred miles in every direction. We were so deep in the woods I couldn't hear the single-lane highway or the hauler trucks, just the sounds of birds.

Pacer gave us cardboard paper targets he bought special for us. He said that he was a cop in a special task force down in Sacramento that trained with homeland security after nine-eleven, when it had become clear that the capitol was a target but that he had to drop out of the taskforce, due to some political machinations at the highest levels that he got wind of and had threatened to expose. Anyway, we got the paper targets set up at his instruction around the dry riverbed. We set three of them in a semi-circle surrounding him, each at forty-five degree angles from one another. They were drawn to look like Taliban insurgents. He told me to yell 'threat' at him three times. So I did that.

Threat. And he fired his silver handgun at a paper target on some rocks in front of him. The warble of ricochet out into the trees. Threat. And a paper insurgent ripped apart at the mouth near some poplars. Threat again and again. Then he told Sho and I to begin resetting his clips, bullet by bullet until our fingers were raw. Then, he gave us both a turn.

When she finally graduated from the Smurf to Pacer's handgun, Pacer showed Sho how to lock her arms at the elbows, straight out in front of her. He showed her from behind her, with Sho's yoga pants so firm against his sagging camouflage cargo pants that I was embarrassed to watch. I focused on reloading magazines but when I checked her expression, Sho didn't seem to mind as much as I did. Each time she squeezed the trigger on Pacer's handgun, Pacer made a face so packed with innuendo I couldn't even force a smile for his benefit. Not even the fake laugh I had perfected. I worried that he was going to see through me again. Like my face was a wet sticker, peeling off at the edges. Then Sho emptied her clip and I knew she didn't need the Smurf lessons.

When I stood where they did, I tried to remember my breathing but my mind was loud with noise. So I thought of nothing. Once, the shooting was a therapy – like guitar practice, fingers up and down a chromatic scale of glitter wire. Pacer and Sho spoke. While I breathed, Pacer asked about her family. I never shot at anyone alive when I was on deployment. While I swept the riverbed for targets, Sho was laughing with him. But I always knew that it would be easy if I had to. Some guys worried about it. Even guys like Pacer, in effusive, desperate confessions they would often reveal that the heroic, me-or-them kill they had bragged about in barracks had never happened. Pacer called them goat stories, because of the way a lot of those made up stories were about the time they had gotten so frustrated and bored with the waiting that they had taken up their ARs and used village goats for target practice. Or dogs. But they were always quick to talk about a hesitation. As if it made them special. Standing there, a civilian again with still no future, no family, I let go and emptied the clip at Pacer's Taliban paper targets, faces billowing on yellow dry rocks in the dirt of the river bed. The valley is full of the sound of brassy ricochets.

When we were done shooting, we wandered out of the dry river bed into a meadow of golden alders, pepper red shrubs coming up from the ground. Sho asked if Los Angeles had any special place as quiet and still as this one. Pacer answered for me. Told her no way and that I was a wanderer even during deployment. He told her that I had made it out with stolen gold and I was only out here on a 'squaw spirit walk' until I could remember where I'd put the bullion. He made throaty calls of native shaman into the trees so that she'd laugh over her beer. But I knew a fake laugh when I saw one by now. The alders shielded us from the wind. Reclining in that tall blood-grass, Pacer drank and said we did good and he knew that we were ready. But later, when we got to his truck, sitting alone by the lake bed, he mentioned Bill Campbell, an old army buddy throwing a poker night out on the lake.

"I'm game," Sho said. "I need a drink and my feet are killing me."

"That's right. Big Raj, come with us." Pacer said.

"Yeah, Raj. We're knocking over a bank at the end of the week." She grinned. "What have you got to lose?"

But Pacer knew that a party with other people would have eaten me whole and taken all the non-thought I had. I realized then, Sho was a stress test of Pacer's devising. To see if I'd run. When they left me at the ranch where I was staying, I looked up in time to see Sho's round face in the passenger window while they turned out onto the highway, his arm around her small shoulders.

III.

Pacer was losing when I met him at the Pink Elephant. Standing behind him, I could see on his monitor he had two cards shy of a flush. When I didn't tell him, he grumbled with uncertainty and redealt the whole hand. The Pink Elephant was a cramped room with a bar on one end and a stage platform in the center with a single pole and a single gel light somewhere in the ceiling's rigging – a cyclops' eye. The walls were cluttered with video poker machines. The Christmas lights together with the tilt mirror panels reflecting the new red carpet made everyone around us the pale-pink color of a throbbing organ.

The place was bullshit, but I had been in a bad mood since shooting with Pacer. Some kind of hangover depressive state that had made me consider crazy thoughts I hadn't thought about for a long time. Four years? Since Katrina, since leaving home again and the drive up the coast until I finally got tired enough to stop in Oregon. Sho's music started to play. I didn't feel anything. I worried I was cracked, or a burn out. But sitting with Pacer made me feel better. If I was a burnout, then Pacer was a twelve-alarm fire.

"What's your impression?" he asked me outside in an enormous blacktop parking lot. A wide open round built for jumping horses and fairgrounds but in that time of night it bore no point of reference, like poured void. There was a bite in the air. All of it smelled like trees. I could see Mount Shasta. Then there was a stray dog trotting from up the street. Pacer was watching me, watching him.

"Small place. How much money could they possibly move through here?"

"Sho says the books are pretty healthy. They gotta have money on-hand to pay out on those big pie-in-the-sky wins. Amirite?"

I didn't know at that moment that he was right. I couldn't imagine anyone winning anything from Pink Elephant except by breaking even with gas money for the drive home. The whole idea felt like a nuisance but I knew I was scared too. And then I thought Pacer sensed it because he said: "Are we gonna do it? You seem a little angry today. And don't take this the wrong way, but Sho said you were acting weird yesterday, too. What's wrong? You spooked?"

"No," I said, snappy. "I'm looking at a sandwich and video poker spot that you're telling me is gonna put us in money. They've been robbed three times, Pacer. Why don't they just leave?"

He laughed hard.

"It's that squaw curse, Big Raj. No one leaves Klamath. We all just swim in it. This is gonna be peanut butter and jelly, Big Raj. Gonna be frosty."

"This isn't like Katrina," I told him. "Cops here care about this place. I don't know why. But they do. And they'll run us down if they get a scent."

"I got a plan for that, too."

We waited until night, talking about Sho in his four-wheel drive, how she was giving him signals that were all woman. Then he got ready for work. He put on a black polo and black baseball cap and a gun belt. I could see how much he loved this job by the way he winked at me. He put on that gun belt and looked in the mirror, and I saw his smile get wide like a shark's. He walked away from the truck in my rearview, didn't check sight-lines. No long looks down the boulevard to see who was there watching. He walked like the mayor. Not a bank robber. Then, I pulled his truck away. After he turned off the cameras at 2:45, I drove back to the Pink Elephant.

Pacer got the door for me.

I took in his green Oregon Ducks vinyl bags, one in either hand and I threw him the materials he asked for, a box of black, surgical gloves. And that felt good because we started to move through the dark down a back hallway into a concrete poured basement. And it wasn't non-thought, but it was close. Pacer had the keys to everything and with those gloves on it was easy, like he was showing me around his house on MTV. In the basement, he showed me the safe. Black with gold trim and four legs that stood with the body raised up off the ground. I didn't know anything about safes but this one looked like a bad one.

When Sho texted I read it out loud, a string of numbers. Pacer moved at my command, his shape at the keypad, the keypad at my disposal until finally a click. Then nothing. I would have laughed if I hadn't been so fucking terrified. My life was effectively placed in Pacer's and Sho's hands, and I didn't think either one legitimately finished high school. But I tried to check myself. Couldn't assume I was above these people. I wasn't.

I had worked on phones for a year and talked to dial-tones from every walk of life and pay scale who still couldn't work a satellite cable box. We were all built the same. All swimming in it together, like Pacer said. Pacer was shouting. He bent over and screamed at the carpet. He went upstairs and back downstairs. And I sat down on the cool ground, because I knew from the night and the way shadows were in that little concrete office, I was either going to be sitting at work tomorrow or in prison for a long time.

We sat like that until Sho texted us again. A new string of

numbers, then more long seconds that we held our breath for. And the safe opened. In the safe, the money was dirty crumpled bills or sorted into baseball rolls beside big bulging white canvas bags.

"No cashier bags. Could have dye packs," I said, but Pacer was already loading them onto his shoulder. I swore at him.

In another few moments we were gone, walking fast behind the Pink Elephant to his truck parked in back. Nothing was around us but the trees and the wind and that enormous blacktop.

At his truck, Pacer's big addition to the plan came into focus. His dramatic 'fuck you' insurance. And it struck me, that in Pacer's mind this would be his 'fuck you' to his bosses when they asked for an alibi. I decided then that it was my 'fuck you' to Pacer, for putting me back in the dark with him, back in the split-second compromises where I inevitably swapped my principles for any way out at all. I could hear the rain again, the way it had been in Katrina. Staccato percussion. And while Pacer was waiting, I grabbed a roll of quarters that had been rolling around his front passenger-seat mat. I packed my fist around it. When I came along the side of his truck to the back, he was red-faced and rushing me.

"Come on come on come on," he said in those little screechy whispers. Pacer squared up. He wanted me to count to three and to pull the punch. But I didn't count to three or pull the punch.

It felt good to see Pacer go down. The long, broad side of him slapped into the glitter of black concrete. So good, that I felt my quads tense and I let a kick explode into Pacer's giant gut. I reached down, digging beneath that hoodie – at his waistband and briefly felt him fight me for his gun. For the clip, full of fat little bullets flashing their teeth at me. I feel like the way I did in the Guard. Back on deployment in the dark water, with private sec guys' spotlights scanning around. Lighting us up through rain. Pacer's gun in my hand feels infinitely heavy, like wet gold washed in greasy rainwater. As if it is filled with our misdeeds. I placed the gun in my pants. I winked at him and he laughed, rolling like a felled over horse, but his mouth was black and wet. And it was a big joke again, the spotlight clicking off in my head forever.

IV.

The next day at work everything was exactly the same on the call center row except for me. I sat and watched my colleagues, upselling DirecTV NFL Sunday Ticket or asking probing questions about the nature of their pixilation. But what was the nature of my pixilation? I dialed into my headset and before the first call came in off my queue , I dialed out to piss.

I checked my Flex Time. Low. It was not just low: it was a decimal value on the spreadsheet. A quarter of a day's work available for time off. A bathroom break maybe, and considering I was dialed out, I had just flushed it again. This was a sustained blow to my metrics. I could expect a 'coaching' from Todd and a review by Quality. All along the row my colleagues were content to be toiling, or talking or typing. And Pacer's cubicle was empty.

At the flavored coffee machine in the breakroom, no one had seen Pacer. Then Todd came in, his mug already uncapped for the coffee. He watched me watch him add convenience store espresso shots. Todd was my supervisor – a large man in a Duck's hat and glasses.

"Did Pacer come in today?" I said.

Todd seemed to consider my question. He weighed me through those thick glasses. Then he said, "You know, I can't actually discuss that information, Raj. But I'll see you out there."

That meant Pacer was probably out. After all his cloak and dagger bullshit, Pacer didn't show up to work the day after his big heist. That, or he had been clipped. If he had been clipped, I was next. I started to have trouble breathing again, and when Howard answered his next call in that cheery DirecTV singsong, I wanted to shout in his red face but I didn't. I practiced non-thought again.

I had learned non-thought in the military. It was the only thing that still worked. Non-thought meant I was not to leave the present moment, for any other moment. I wasn't thinking about Pacer's handgun in my glovebox in my car outside because I was at my desk. It meant I didn't think of Sho not being at work either because I had my headset on and was sitting at my computer. It meant I definitely did not think that if I got up and left for California now I would still have the rest of my life, free and ungridded by a DirecTV spreadsheet. So I stood up and locked my drawer and forgot my coat.

In my Corolla, I managed to regain some kind of composure. I checked on Pacer's handgun. It was still sitting on my registration, beside the American Spirits I kept in my glovebox. But I shut that because across our call center lot, I could see Sho talking to Rex, our county sheriff's deputy who always let you off with a warning if he caught you doing anything low-level stupid like blowing lights.

She looked bad. One of her eyes was swollen. Makeup in streaks coming down her face. Our worthless human resource manager, with big hair, was at her heels when Sho got into her grandmother's four-wheel Tacoma going the opposite way. The door slammed hard enough to make the cardboard on the back window shake. Then human resources just stood there in the hard wind and watched them both go. Human resources and I watched, worthless together.

When I got to Sho's side of the river between the tracks of trailers, she was in a hoodie and walking around outside her grandmother's place. The swelling had receded into the purple bubble of her inflamed eye socket but I didn't ask. Grandma didn't say hi to me, while a gaggle of kids and parents milled about the wide open suburban streets trick-or-treating in white ghost sheets, or as green Frankenstein-monsters. The houses in the trailer park were well-kept with fresh coats of paint and railroad tie steps that led up to pretty white doors. They looked like a good set of teeth in a rotting mouth. I didn't spend a lot of time on this side of the lake, so I was surprised to see how close the properties ran to the water. They could walk right up to the ducks and lilies, a dream.

When Sho saw me, she looked away. I felt a strong ray of anger cut through my numb haze. Like I was just as bad as Pacer. Like I was complicit.

"You feel like walking?" I asked.

"Yah," she said.

"Is this your costume?"

"I'm a teen-aged bank robber."

"It's not very good."

Just like that I saw her smile. We walked until we got to the interstate. Until I, almost too late, understood the charm of this place. We were all swimming in it together. Like a repository for all the hopeless pieces on the West Coast that just did not make it anywhere else. Everything broken flowed to Klamath Falls. They pumped the gas for one another, sometimes terrorized or saved one another. I thought I was really getting it when Sho told me about Bill's poker party on the lake last night.

The party had run late when Pacer showed up talking loud about the Pink Elephant. Then he got rough and handsy in front of Bill, who tried to get them apart. It was almost light out when Pacer drove away. Then, he found her later on the road and drove her home and passed her home, and Sho got scared at the way he was speeding. He had sped almost all the way to Chilloquin by the time she got her door open and jumped.

"I wish you'd have told me about him," she said.

"So do I," I said.

"I want to kill him."

"Me too," I said.

She seemed as if she didn't believe me. So I said it again. Sho and I had stolen twenty-four thousand dollars from the Pink Elephant. We were both thinking the same thing. You couldn't really blame us. So I laid out a plan B.

"Pacer gave me three-thousand last night. He said he would move the rest and launder it slowly. If I don't leave soon it's going to be too hard to get back to Los Angeles later. That money will just burn up." I could see that she understood that I really meant that I would burn up.

"Will you take me?" she says.

"What about, Pacer? What about the money?"

"It doesn't matter anymore."

"Okay," I said.

"Okay?" she said "What are you and I going to do in Los Angeles? This some kind of fairytale to you?"

"There are call centers in Los Angeles, you know?" I said. She looked at me again, so I said, "There are strip clubs in Los Angeles, you know. And besides, you don't have to be with me. Me and you. You could split when we get out there."

She had her fake stiletto thumbnail in her mouth, looking equal parts afraid and intrigued. I realized that I still didn't feel anything. I realized that I didn't feel cold and I didn't feel the walk back to her house. I didn't even feel her kiss me on the cheek and tell me to wake her up with a phone call before I came over to pick her up in the morning. And even when I agreed and the light of her doorway narrowed and shut on me, I knew that I wouldn't see her again. So I practiced non-thought. Non-thought while I drive the backroads to avoid police. Non-thought while I hunt for Pacer.

In the morning, I got up before anyone else on the ranch. The ground was frozen in the first snowfall of winter with the Trakkeners and Appaloosas running in those slow floating trots, tossing their manes in pony circles to keep warm maybe. And I try digging at the spot by the edge of the paddock until the unvarnished shovel bites into my hand, splits and breaks its neck in the ice. So I leave the bullion there for some lucky landscaper, or kid digging a hundred years from now.

My Corolla brayed at me, starting unsteady and kicking in stop-starts. I drove to Sho, who had already texted twice that she was up and awake. She had wanted to know whether I wanted coffee or just Red Bull for the long drive out. That she was happy and had been so excited and without sleep. That she had gone out and gotten all of it, plus some salt water taffy. And I drove to her lake where those trailer park lights were coming on opal against the pink purple morning. And the transmission finally caught, and the wheels fell in-line with the road and I sailed beyond the lake, passed the burnt down lots with high grass toward the edge of town where the brick call center stood on a hill near the trucking roads. And I went to work and took calls until the world regained equilibrium.

In the gray linoleum lunch room by the coffee machine, those of us on porn calls shift had started mentally preparing for the long silence of downtime at the center. Porn time. Then Robert sat down at my table and said, "Happy November, I guess." And he laughed. Was it already November? I nodded anyway.

Robert was a black kid from my training class with a bright blue gaze and braces. He was deeply Christian with a penchant for pointing out moral inadequacies in others, so he did not get invited to Campbell's or to lunch breaks by the smoking area. But we both served and tonight it was just us in the lunch room. I made eye-contact, inviting him.

"Iraq," he said with a shrug. "Porn calls remind me of deployment. We used to get so riled up and bored out there. One night my friend, Cecil, and I went out and grabbed some blocks of C4. There was this shepherd we had to yell at every day to get back out from our perimeter. This guy was deaf or stupid because every night sure as shit he was there with his damn goats. So we took these blocks and got one of his goats isolated from the rest. We put so much C4 on that goat it was like a thunder clap. Only thing left was the bell."

I gave him my fake laugh. I closed my eyes and brought my shoulders up. Like my whole body was a laughing spasm. I put in some sounds. And I hit the table. When I opened up my eyes Robert was looking back at me. I cleaned my place-setting. I went to my cubicle. I practiced non-thought.

People Say

People say, "Get help" when you are sad and down. People say, "Don't suffer in secrecy and alone." People say so much, and most of what they say is BS. "He wouldn't have to try to kill himself if he had sought some professional help", they say. Maybe he did seek professional help but some troubled professional helper with complicated letter combination such as PhD, MD, MS, NCC, LPC, LMF, LMFC, LCSW-R, etc. after his name was so emotionally overwhelming to him, he had to kill himself. Maybe he couldn't handle one more narcissistic bipolar sociopath professional helper. Maybe he realized that PhD, MD, or whatever title, doesn't guarantee you are not a psychopath who hates the human race and who suffocates his clients with BS he keeps pouring in those suffering little throats asking for help.

People said he jumped out of the 5th floor window, but he wasn't meant to die. The neighbors said he landed on a vintage Citroen and didn't even break a bone. They said he had a concussion only. They all said it was a miracle he was alive.

Maybe after a tedious day of work helping crazy and suicidal people, the professional helper goes home, walks the dog, has an alcoholic beverage, hates his wife and kids, and fucks the neighbor's pre-menopausal wife. Maybe he does. That's what I have heard. People talk so much.

Marja Hagborg

Weird Kid with a Red Yankee Bag: Red

One Sunday morning my paternal grandfather rode his horse into the village church. He kept riding until he reached the altar yelling some drunken nonsense about how the world was huge and he was following only his own rules. The parish clerk gently and politely showed the horse and my mindlessly drunk grandfather the way out.

My mother, who had nothing good to say about my father or his relatives, told me about my grandfather's church visit. According to her, they all were evil alcoholics, grandiose, self-centered and narcissistic bullies, and I should be careful because I could easily become one of them. Alcoholism is believed to jump over every other generation; my father didn't drink, he was, as my mother put it, simply an asshole from birth.

I hardly knew my father, I saw him only once or twice a year. To me he seemed like a confused tomcat when meeting his own offspring, not knowing what to do, to piss on them or clean their butts. He was a lost old man, entirely occupied by his own thoughts, chain-smoking and protecting brooding birds on his tiny island. His wife used to look at me as if I were a zoo animal, a rabid monkey wearing clothes only dangerous city kids wear.

I loved the island, but only as an idea in my head, not actually being there. I loved its sighing pine trees, its soft moss under my bare feet, the warm west wind, the lake that was often covered by silvery light, small perches swimming near the surface close to the rocks where I used to sit and plan my escape. I always had the compulsion to leave as soon as I had arrived, but I tried to stay long enough to inhale the intoxicating lake air and take mental pictures for the future.

My father and his wife used to watch me through the kitchen window, she possibly asking my father what his weird kid was doing, just sitting on the rocks and hanging her feet in the lake.

What was wrong with her? Weird like her mother! I felt her eyes, her eye; she actually had only one functioning eye, in my back.

After I had walked around the island letting my bare feet sink into the soft green moss, listening to the wind and the birds, watching the small perches in the water for awhile, I took my red Yankee bag and told my father I had stomachache and I had to get home because I had to see a doctor. I may have been dying. When sitting in the bus on my way back to the city, I immediately felt better seeing the village behind me, and the landscape rolling by faster and faster. Every minute I was closer to home.

Marja Hagborg

Martello Tower

It was many years ago now
it was June 5, 1993 –
I wasn't young, already
    middling, but free.

Free to go
so I took myself to Dublin –
It seemed proper –

    I'd been reading
Ulysses and it begins
at the Martello tower, just

on the dingle coast, a poor
beach, a dim morning –
not a tour stop then –

they'd just whitewashed
inside – the taxi man
thought me daft

    but there was
a gift shop at the bottom
I left my cane there

to have hands free
for whitewashed walls
Looking up into

sea mist, where
part of the upstairs went
missing, but steps

I wanted to see
what the young men saw
    who slept there –

no beds, no desks
(trimmings added later
I'm told) but a cash register.

A hole where the floor
went missing, but steps up
Up , the only way to go

and I did it, determined
bad knee and all
to see what they saw

when I hauled myself out
at the top, I found
a flat roof, or a perch

an airy place
for observations popular
for half-blind eyes

doing research, perhaps
into "snot-green," fit
for foggy water.

Ruth Moon Kempher

Sparks Fly

right in the center of the picture called:
Sympathy formerly
The Madness of the Cat

centered, the cat is a long, arched-back orange
creature, electric its hair is like fish bones
a curved filet, spinal, it's

another Remedios Varo oil painting
and the cat flies over the table, milk spills
from the orange cloth where a glass dumped

and the lady seated at the table's head
has hair zapped into new, permanent waves –
doesn't look like Remedios

but probably is. She preferred cats
to people. First titled the painting a word
like *Rabies*. Changed it to be *Simpatico*

You have to look close to see
there's another cat, weaving under the table
deep in shadows. Hiding what it thinks.

Ruth Moon Kempher

All Utopias Fell 2, Michael Oatman, MASS MoCA

We start with words

Know there should be more
      even an abstract painting where desert grit
      is mixed with tan and turquoise
      spread on plywood because no canvas can hold it
      no brushes   only hands to apply

I play Georgia O'Keeffe
      and you Hank Williams in a theatre for 500
audience small for a performance
that spans time   and space

Someone stands at a piano far from the keys
      top of the upright open   and plucks strings

We march across an empty stage
      but every time the pianist claps his hands
      we change directions

We decide this is enough.

Kyle Laws

All Utopias Fell 3, Michael Oatman, MASS MoCA

We reside in *The Library of the Sun*
      books floor to ceiling strapped in with belts
      as packs on burros on the way down
      the Grand Canyon
      we spend nights on separate cots
      hands reaching across the divide
      of north and south rim
      between us runs the river to California
      that falls off La Poudre Pass
      330 days of sun burns at high elevations
      there is not a hat with wide enough brim
      nothing to stop the spell of this much time with books
      nothing to keep me from crawling to the other side
      and trying to share a narrow bed.

Kyle Laws

All Utopias Fell 4, Michael Oatman, MASS MoCA

In a year of no heat –
out my bitter studio window
parachutes flag where they once unfurled.

Empty trains rumble by past midnight
and the woman in the next apartment cries
and coughs through the second night in a row.

I worry over losing a rag torn
from the bottom of your shirt to wipe glasses
find it in the bottom of a suitcase of summer clothes.

While you die slowly in another state
I see you in every work of art in the cavernous museum.
To keep warm I write one more love poem.

Kyle Laws

Saturday Movies

Before movies with boys
trying to put their hands in
under angora or a felt
jumper and after the
endless westerns, dust,
hats and hooves pounding,
boring we thought, sucking
on Junior Mints, it was
the movies with stars
we ached to be. Vera Ellen
with a 16 inch waist,
Pier Angeli pale and shy
Photoplay said, in a
peasant dress I cut out and
put on my wall near the
cinch belted Vera,
stood near my mother's
mirror with my waist pulled
in, sucking myself into
myself as if I could
swallow my pink glasses,
little paunch. I never wanted
to be Marilyn Monroe,
Jane Russell or Jayne
Mansfield women with huge
hips, breasts but Audrey
Hepburn slim, able to slip in
to a new life, escape from
my grandfather sneakily
lurking behind me at
parties or the movies. I
wanted to wear postage size
cashmere, pale and silvery
shoes I could balance
forever in, suspended on
toes that could brush your
skin while you slept,

hover around your quilt, a
movie queen angel you'd
wake to the dazzling glow of,
wild to keep and hold

As Children

she was the beauty, I
was the one who won
science contests and
got good grades but
didn't get asked out
or given watches. I'm
blonder than she'll
ever be but our long
hair is braided with
sadness that nothing
can unsnarl

In that House, Light thru Dripping Icicles

apricot beads. My forehead
against red wood frame glass
before scars. Knives before
tango knifed its stain in ruby
drugs, indelible as the deepest
tongue wild for more

Lyn Lifshin

She Says Her 'Friend' She Calls Him That. He Lives with Her and Her Husband

but its "friend" she always says but never
her or his friend. Or his name. She gives me
details of his days, what color he wears each day
but never a name. Was he a former love? A
love? Her husband's lover? But never mentions
his name. Or if he's from Dakota or Montana?
The plot of a movie I'd seen. She unravels
the hours of the 3 days she didn't write me. 17
pages and a 3 page PS. The people she brings
food to in the park who love her long pre chemo
braids to her waist. The print is 8 pages. I could
never read each letter and still write words of my
own. I ask her, I know she is busy and stressed but
I ask her for a blurb but to say no if she just
doesn't have the energy to do it. It's fine
and she writes me "Can you tell me who
wrote it and a little about it"

Lyn Lifshin

untitled

This morning she tells me
she dreamt she was a Japanese
porn star. What happened, I
ask? I was waiting in a room
for him to finish, so he could
cum, she says. That was it. I
imagine her as a Japanese porn
star. She looks like a cat already,
with very dark, diagonal eyes.
Cleopatra without need of ash.
I don't know Japanese but I
imagine it would sound beautiful.
KUREOPATRA. I imagine she
would take the Japanese porn
world by storm. Likely the entire
industry. And then crossover to
mainstream movies.
KUREOPATRA, X porn star,
bored but willing. Oh my love,
she says, like a cat, and then goes
back to sleep. Back to her cat
world. Her diagonal eyes closed,
her dark lashes draped atop her
moon white face. The great
kaleidoscope is turning. It's a
new day.

Anthony Lucero

Sarah Daugherty

A Conversation with klipschutz

Born in Indio, CA, klipschutz (pen name of Kurt Lipschutz) left high school early to travel the U.S. by thumb, then lived in Laurel Canyon, Echo Park, and Hollywood, where he wrote stand-up comedy, before a short stint at Naropa. First marriage, San Francisco, Gallup polls (door-to-door), first fruits: *The Erection of Scaffolding for the Re-Painting of Heaven by the Lowest Bidder* (o.p.). Recently, he was shocked to discover that he has published six previous collections. His latest collection is *Premeditations* (2019, Hoot n Waddle Press).

As well, he has co-written approximately 100 songs released by Chuck Prophet, whose latest is *The Land That Time Forgot* (2020). With Jeremy Gaulke, between 2014 and 2017, klipschutz edited the collectible mini-mag *Four by Two* through twelve issues. (A complete set resides in the Special Collections Library at U.C. Berkeley.) He lives in San Francisco with Colette Jappy and three tuxedo cats.

*****

SARAH: Tell us about yourself and how creative expression became a necessity to you.

KLIPSCHUTZ: My oldest brother populated his bookshelves with Henry Miller, Bukowski, Celine, and the Beats. Looking back, pretty male, hetero, and white (except for Bob Kaufman and Diane di Prima). But that was the world back then. This was maybe 1969. Add Bob Dylan to the mix and I was off to the races. Where exactly the urge came from and how it has sustained – that I don't want to know, but it came early on. Maybe it's in my DNA, or the fluoride in the water.

SARAH: Given your contacts and collaborations with musicians, what drew you to writing poetry instead of being in the bands?

KLIPSCHUTZ: Well, I have a temperamental bladder, and wouldn't have lasted three gigs in a touring van, so there's that.

Also, poetry came into my orbit before music. Plus, my piano teacher dropped me for abundant cause. Songwriting came when I saw Bone Cootes busking on Haight Street. About four years later, Bone and I wrote a song with Chuck Prophet, and Chuck hasn't been able to shake me since.

SARAH: And what made you focus on writing for and editing small press publications, instead of pursuing mainstream publications?

KLIPSCHUTZ: The mainstream seems to be allergic to me. I had two pieces in *Poetry* (of Chicago) in 1992, but they have not seen fit to repeat their mistake. And Wesleyan University Press toyed with me hard in 1994 before coming to their senses. Ditto City Lights. Overall, I've danced with the ones who would have me.

SARAH: You are one of my favorite small press poets to read. I like the humor and quick pace of your writing; your poems are smart, lively, and always entertaining.

So now, for my question(s): In this era of constant media distraction, what is the significance of a poem? Why do you think there is an upsurge of popular interest in poetry?

KLIPSCHUTZ: Well, thanks and thanks again. Poets crave praise like a dog likes to hear his or her name! Good questions, but you should know that by now – I'm 64 – I don't think about the big topics like 'significance' much. And to tell you the truth, the upsurge you mention I'm not sure I've even noticed. To me, the poetry world is kind of like my neighborhood in San Francisco, the Tendernob, on the cusp of the Tenderloin and Nob Hill. We get upscale aspects (craft ice cream!), but homeless people still sleep in our doorway. There are tents on the street, and artisanal beer. Both situations are real, side by side. I think that's what Keats called 'negative capability.'

So, I guess the way I think of it is that good and bad things are happening all the time. Are the Instagram Poets a positive development? Is Rupi Kaur 'good' for poetry? It depends who you ask, and since you're asking me, my take is 'no.' It's ersatz. Disposable. Then there's the incursion of Identity Politics into poetry. Since I'm a straight, cisgender white male, and old, I'm part of the demographic that Eileen Myles said in an interview should just shut up and not write or publish anything for the next 50 years. Am I allowed to disagree? It's the poem, isn't it, not the name on it, or the biographical particulars of who wrote it? But, people do seem to be more interested, if not life-changingly so, in my own poems lately. Which I couldn't be happier about.

SARAH: And what is the purpose of a poem in the current U.S. culture? Is it for entertainment? Political commentary? Deep-deep-thinky stuff? Or is poetry primarily a tool for people to *seem* bookish? (An idea comparable to a person wearing eyeglasses to seem bookish, if that's still a thing.) And what do you think poetry is for?

KLIPSCHUTZ: All of the above! Poetry has an uphill battle. Entertainment: We're in competition with comedians and talk show hosts. And it's a golden age for them. Poets are hamstrung by political correctness. Sure, comedians get in hot water, but some are fearless. (Eric Andre!) Poets, editors, publishers, not so much. Political commentary: We have stiff competition there too, on many fronts. For people who remember, the great Hunter T. Thompson combined literary heft, journalistic flow, slashing humor, and informed, biting analysis. While there's no one quite like him now, again, some of the late-nite talk show hosts are keeping it real.

Deep-thinky stuff: I'll go with Bukowski, who said an intellectual can take a simple idea and make it complicated and an artist can take a complex idea and cut to the chase. (Or words to that effect). As to posers, with or without glasses, same as it ever was. And on what poetry is for – can I get back to you in about 10 years? I may need to hire an expert. And experts are expensive, so I should start saving. I will say, though, and this colors what I've just said, that there are things and approaches poetry can do better than stand-up or YouTube or songs or films or paintings. In other words, something a comic or commentator can't! That's a heavy lift, but it's also a natural fact. And for me it's a know-it-when-I-see it deal more than a definition or a prescription.

SARAH: That's cool, even though 'know-it-when-I see-it' can also add an oddness to an artist's side life. As a writer myself, I notice that sometimes my friends and family are nervous that I have written or will write about them. I don't write overtly confessional poetry, so it's easy for me to say, 'My poetry usually isn't about anything real. Images and thoughts just come out and mentally connect as a poem.' This is the easy answer, and I'm sticking to it, but I know that real life is part of that mental connection. I call it 'seepage,' but only when I am alone. It's just that, even if subdued, real life people, experiences, events, or perspectives vivify and even create poems.

So based on that, tell me a story. Tell me about a specific event, or a personal experience or insight you had, and then explain how it 'seeped' (overtly or covertly) into a poem, even if the seepage only influenced voice or perspective. Explain the changes that you made (exaggerations, contortions, deletions) to the event or experience to make them match the mental connections intended for the poem. Or, from your story example, did you play with the ideas and images until a poem was connected and shaped?

KLIPSCHUTZ: First off, a quote from Czeslaw Milosz: 'When a poet is born into a family, that family is finished.' I haven't completely finished my family off yet, but I'm making steady progress! Okay, then, multiple examples come to mind of seepage. I'll leave my family out of this one – they've suffered enough – and stick to two friends.

'Love & Kisses,' a suite of five poems, is the centerpiece of *Premeditations*. The protagonist is Carol Tinker, Kenneth Rexroth's widow and a poet and painter in her own right. Around the Y2K Scare, we met at a reading in Santa Barbara, where she lived, and she kind of adopted me. She took to my poems and we were both phone people. Late at night she'd call and give me endless advice. At first, I thought she might have some connections, but I soon found out she was a recluse and had gone to the same charm school as me. Carol would tell me everything I was reading was wrong, and what I should read instead. She was brilliant, and maybe something of a drinker. Hilariously dismissive when she wanted to be.

She died in 2012, so she never got to see 'Love and Kisses,' which quotes her lavishly. It started when I began to write down what she was saying on the phone – major seepage! – especially since she held court and my role was basically to listen, be playfully berated, and praised if I agreed with her. Parts of the poems take the form of impressionistic phone transcripts. Overall I don't think it's unflattering, but I doubt she would agree. Besides, for me the poems were about creating a *version* of her, not Carol herself. In the process of rearranging and selecting, some exaggeration was inevitable. And the first poem in the series, a prose poem, I made up entirely. On the confessional tip, I will admit to settling a score with a mutual acquaintance Carol mentions, Patrick (his real name). Carol seemed to take a strange pleasure in telling me how fat he was getting. And so did I – so I put that in. Patrick is about fifteen years younger than I am. A while back, he had turned on me, and called me a 'mediocre middle-aged poet.' Then, since he has mental health issues, he thought we could still be pals.

SARAH: In keeping with that line of thought, but on a more general level. What is your writing process?

KLIPSCHUTZ: Visions and revisions, like T.S. Eliot said. And more revisions. And then some more. Time and distance. Lack of sleep to induce one more finishing push. Sometimes a poem takes me twenty years, and then I go back to the original first draft. My poems start from lines, not ideas. And I don't like to know where the poem is going. If I surprise myself, I have at least a fighting chance to keep the reader engaged. That's a paraphrase of Frost.

SARAH: In your new book, I notice that you refer to a number of canonical poets in the titles (including Wallace Stevens, Robinson Jeffers, Kay Ryan), in-text references, and allusions. Yet you bring them into contemporary relevance often using a humorous lens. Was it your intent to humanize modern canonical poets and contemporize their works? Or were the poems in which you allude to these works intent on capturing your reactions and interpretations of the poems as you apply them to your perspectives and these times? Or both?

KLIPSCHUTZ: Poems come from life, and sometimes poems come from life by way of other poems and from reading and absorbing poets, loving and hating them, arguing with them, correcting them, stealing from them, paying homage. Kay Ryan has a distinctive style and I was moved to address her in it, to mimic and honor her at the same time. Robinson Jeffers is a strange and problematic figure, an *isolato* and a political conservative whose poems about hawks and wind and cliffs and unruly waves were embraced by the Sierra Club. I got a kick out of picturing him as a one-man band, like you see at tourist spots, the guy playing a ukulele while beating a kick drum with his feet and shaking a tambourine he wears like a crown. He can do it all, only he needs you, the audience, to toss coins in his hat in order to be able to eat the next day. Similarly, Jeffers needed an audience, and for many years he actually had one. Bukowski revered him.

Wallace Stevens, I feel duty bound to point out, was a stone cold racist, and also an anti-Semite. But one of the most sublime philosophical poets of all time, I'll step out on a limb and declare. My poem for him was originally four separate ones. In parts of it I'm channeling him. Also, both the Jeffers and Stevens poems are in a way impressionistic sketches, sort of like those portraits Calder did with wire of figures like Fernand Léger and Josephine Baker.

SARAH: Based on this, how important is literary tradition? I teach English, and I always tell my students that before Steinbeck or Hemingway were on required college English reading lists, they were popular writers who wrote books that people wanted to read. Even Shakespeare wrote plays to sell tickets. As a poet with a background of Beat poetry influences, influences considered deviant from the literary norm, what do you think of the value of poetry simply because it's 'good' regardless from which the poetic movement or era it came?

KLIPSCHUTZ: 'Good' is a tough one. If you'll allow me to substitute 'appealing,' that I can roll with. Leaving out the thorny issue of appealing to whom. I am attracted to a wide variety of writing, which includes characters like Raymond Chandler, who wrote pulp novels that stuck around – which is Frost's definition of a great poem: one you can't get rid of. Chandler stuck around long enough to get grandfathered into the canon. Again, in deference to the times, I feel compelled to point out that he was also a king hell racist (*Farewell My Lovely* in particular), and no slouch as a homophobe and anti-Semite. Maybe, though, if I may suggest, we can stop holding writers to a strict standard of belief systems and judge them on the totality of their books, or even their styles. Or else we can purge our bookshelves and leave only Alice Walker. But oops! She's also an anti-Semite, so it looks like the French Revolution all over again once heads start to roll.

SARAH: In *Premeditations* there are poems about established poets that evoke blues standards, such as 'A' Comin' and 'Alfred Fowler (Kayo) Saxton,' or that reference folk or country music traditions, such as 'Instructor's Critique' and 'Autumnal.' What is your intention with these choices? And from your perspective, what roles do the blues and folk and jazz music traditions have in the world (and future) of poetry? And in the world in general?

KLIPSCHUTZ: I try not to have intentions. Leonard Cohen said that our opinions are the least interesting thing about us. And Lord knows I have plenty of opinions. (Colette sure knows that!) When it comes to writing, though, I am as likely to channel another voice or point of view as I am to lay out my own. As to music, I'm also a songwriter, primarily with Chuck Prophet, so I've co-written blues, folk, country, and rock tunes. Jazz is a ways out of my wheelhouse, though I appreciate it. Songs are songs and poems are poems, except when they aren't. Like Ray Davies says in 'Lola': 'It's a mixed up, muddled up, shook up world,' and that goes double for music and poetry! When a songwriter wins the Nobel Prize for Literature, all bets are off.

SARAH: I agree. Songs are often more accessible than poems. So I wonder: how important is the accessibility of meaning in poetry? As a poet and someone who reads poetry, which of the following do you think to be true of 'good' poetry: 1) the poem's meaning is wide open; 2) the poem's meaning is guided, yet open to interpretation; and/or 3) the poem's meaning is fixed?

KLIPSCHUTZ: Accessibility as it refers to poetry is a double-edged sword. It's a put-down as often as it's a praise word. Just ask Billy Collins. I like my poems clear on the surface, with mystery lurking underneath and woven inside of them. That goes for the poems I write and the poems I like to read. As to door number 1, 2, or 3, I hate to sound too agreeable, but I think all three are true. It depends on the poem. To me, chasing meaning is a game, and often not as amusing as Twister or as exhausting as a disagreement with Sharon Doubiago, whose poems and prose I highly recommend. But I don't teach, and I don't want to put you and other teachers out of work. so far be it from me to interfere with the hunting of the snark …

SARAH: Well, I wear many hats: teacher, poet, editor are a few among many, and sometimes I forget to change hats! However, in this discussion, the hat that suits me best is 'poetry lover,' and I think this same hat fits all of the *Chiron* readers, including the poets themselves. I honestly don't know of anyone who writes poetry because they hate poetry – but that's another interview with a poet who has yet to come forward!

But back to you – I have said this many times before: I really like your poetry. Your writing has consistently enjoyable surface value; your poems are clever and true, imagistic but precise. And then there is always the intentional deeper meaning, which is your aim, as you just said. I am happy that your poems have appeared in *Chiron Review* and I am really pleased to be able to speak with you in this interview so that *Chiron* readers can find out more about you and your work! That said, I am having difficulty ending our fun talk, but it has to close up somehow ... So I've decided to end it swiftly, to cut it like a guillotine. Before I do so, any last words?

KLIPSCHUTZ: I think I'll just bask in your generosity and appreciation. After all these years, when we finally meet, the first few rounds are on me.

SARAH: It's been a great talk, Kurt! And when you say the 'first few rounds' are on you whenever we actually meet, I will hold you to that. But I hope you mean three booze drinks followed by black coffee … because I'm an enthusiastic lightweight with caffeine needs! Thanks in advance – and thanks for the interview and for sharing some of your poems in this edition of *Chiron Review*!

Coda Red

Do not mistake her thighs for appletrees,
her knees for A, her ankles B.
Does our lady have a vial of ambergris?
Not having seen the inside of her purse,
of her cottage, of her fridge or her ashtray,
best not to speculate. And yet, perhaps.
A bowl of lilacs is not out of the question.
A mandrake root misplaced beneath her bed.
The unmown lawn I did see, from a car,
waiting for her to appear. In August,
she coughs hard, sans explanation.
Ash is in the air, drifting down like snow.
The foothills glow. A summer fire, northwest
of Santa Barbara, the price for death-defying calm,
for sun nine months a year, kingfisher weather.
Calm? It is defined by its exceptions,
much as she is built out of her quirks.
All this and more is her.

klipschutz

Nightmare: I'm the Last Beatnik at the Caffè Trieste – and I Rhyme

"I wake up from dream to dream, the bells! the bells!
of the Church of Saints Peter and Paul"

It might not be the scene for you
The wine is red, the palette blue
Colors bleed, at least some do
   into my little boho life

Cornered spiders set up shop
Raincoat hangs on handle mop
Bills and canvas pile up
   with plates of pork fried rice

No car, one cat, what family?
The boys next door look in on me
There's more and less than what you see
   to how I roll the dice

My landlord wants me gone and soon
He must be all of thirty-two
He's never even seen High Noon –
   a steal at half the price

His tee shirt blazons Fight the Power
He picks up phone calls in the shower
Informs me my "lifestyle" is why
   his zazen room has mice

    Ex-wives drop by, employed, re-wed
Some hungers are best left unfed
There's barely room for one in bed
    besides I'm not my type

Verse Reply from *The Etruscan Review*

If there *were* such a world,
You might find refuge there.

    As it stands, you remain
Rhythmically adrift

    On the table-wine-dark sea
Of mitochondrial lament.

    Back, the wind blows back
Your dirge-like promises

    And threats, disharmonies
That by osmosis breed.

    Feel free to stir wet ashes,
But give wide berth to us.

klipschutz

I'm sure a carpenter

it's funny – I know people
for whom I've never
written poems.
and it's not
because they're boring –
it's just I'm bad
at craft. some people you can't
get right
sometimes.
so you don't try
at any time.

certain trees, I'm sure a carpenter
would say are bad
for building tables.
but still, they
are beautiful
as trees.

DS Maolalai

Lorca's Gaze

your
moon
bruise –
blue
rush
of
words
knocked
me
over
playing
dead
in
outlines
of
seaweed
and
shells –
they
soaked
me
through
to
emptied
silence –
pages
of
foam
where
you
curled
up
next
to
me –
the
only

trace
you
were
not
a
dream
are
your
light
bird
tracks
from
my
heart
to
the
sea

Alicia Mathias

Baby Boomers

Our parents belonged to the Greatest Generation;
ours was the Age of Aquarius. Optimism
was the air we breathed. Our parents fought
The Great War; we stopped a war with sit-ins,
marches (and yes, too many deaths).

We saw civil rights extend to the descendants
of slaves. We saw freedom and equality come
to women, saw that our daughters would be able
to love as freely as men, nearly without consequence.

We would never sacrifice our lives to the tyranny
of the dollar. Our lives would have meaning.

We danced at drum circles.
We showered each other with flowers.
We burned our bras.
We expanded our minds with drugs and philosophy.

Now we limp around on tired knees. We sing and sway
in concert halls where our remaining rock idols croak
in life-graveled voices. We nibble on the crumbs
the Establishment has left for us: Ativan, Viagra,
and legal marijuana.

Tamara Madison

Flesh Remembers

They chopped down the sycamore. I watched a man
feed the tree's weeping flesh to a grinder, flesh so red
I expected bone to poke out white, accusing.

When they pruned the pine tree, they hacked
the branches, leaving each one red on the end,
welling with sap that fell to the ground like tears.

I tripped over a stump by a campfire last summer.
The gash on my shin was a chasm bleeding black
in the dark. My flesh remembers that camping trip –

cold rushing water, nights bright with stars, redwoods
like gigantic buildings, my companion asleep
at nightfall, and me in the dark, wet flesh weeping.

Tamara Madison

The Nicest Man

Near the end, all his fierceness
is gone. Stroke-softened, trembling
from Parkinson's, mind veiled
by dementia, this boulder of a man
whose temper terrorized employees
and family alike, spends his days
hunched before the TV watching
M*A*S*H reruns and the Iran-Contra
hearings (*I've always been a Republican,
but now I'm not so sure*, he tells me).
One morning I find the TV tuned to PBS.
Dad! You're watching Mr. Rogers!
The frightening vehemence back
in his face, he turns to me and growls,
THAT is the NICEST man!

Tamara Madison

Homemade Vegetable Soup

Why did I so dislike my mother's prized
vegetable soup, tomato rich, celery
wealthy, affluent with cabbage, opulent
in peas and carrots, potatoes, onions,
occasional chunks of gristly beef?

Stingy eater, I don't remember ever quite
altogether breaking my mother's heart
over her famous soup, but today,
decades later, I am haunted by
what I would not bring myself to
spoon into my maw for love or money.

Only diced potatoes and scraps of lean beef
and a couple slurps of vitamin-rich broth
sustained me to my next peanut butter sandwich.

From her grave beside my father in Belmont County,
my mother's cold, dry ashes, could they complain,
would reprimand me, starved for affection.

Ron McFarland

Chika Onyenezi

Water

"Water has no enemy." – Yoruba proverb

We are born to drown. To wade through invisible waters until we are no more. Each breath is an air bubble sipping through us, and like in underwater, we exhale to stay alive. We beat against the current, we beat against the realities of our street. We beat and beat until we give up. I saw it happen to someone before. She was my friend. She was fine at the beginning of the year, and like a seed eaten by weevils, she shriveled and died and was buried a week after her death. The heart-wrenching sight of a casket seating at the back of a brown Volvo wagon car, siren blaring and driving into our yard. We watched with tears in our eyes, and the cemented floor was covered with black seeds and fallen leaves. Dust. Dust trailed the wagon from pothole to pothole down the unpaved path and towards her village for final internment. God rest her soul. I watched the car head towards a meeting point of sky and green grass and wondered who would be next. Who would be next? I was eighteen when that wagon pulled in and all I could remember was how many dreams we shared together. That someone with so much to live for and aspirations and longings and longings could just give up after fighting for almost a year, was something that altered my perspective of life, it made me wonder the point of it all. But again, what's the point of it all? These days, whenever I drive through a cemetery, I see my future, to be earthed and slabbed with stone. The minty smell a river hovering above us, and drawing all the birds to its arm. Palms. tall palms whispering lullabies by the riverfront. I let my bucket into the river and scooped water with it. I thought about the casket while balancing the bucket on my head. I walked the small unpaved path carrying water and tried to avoid the spare grasses. It was a routine then because the pipe water rarely runs even though the bills arrived monthly. Whatever happened, we found a way to carry on.

The uncurated symphony of crickets and frogs filled the

night, and every other night it rained. The rain ran through an uncarved path on the road and emptied debris into the river. The corn stalks were tall with combs and a beehive formed on the oha tree, right in the middle of our farm. It wasn't a good omen for bees to form near a house. Father came back home drenched in sweat, dragging his motorcycle in silence, his eyes shot red by sadness. That machine broke almost all the time, and torment of repairs must have emptied him. Mother was under the bush butter tree, smiling and watching her chickens peck food. The seeds on the tree were ready for harvest – the thought of roasting them in a fire with corn made my mouth watery. Mother had chaplet in her hand, she moved them, bead by bead. Hail Mary full of grace. Her salvation. Her hope for eternity. Her hope for a final resting place in heaven. The weight of reality wasn't something to be faced without the help of God. These things kept us alive. These things kept us waiting. Everyone on our street was waiting for salvation, one way or another. Ah, that flowing water of God from which we all drank from. We were thirsty enough to hunger for redemption from our tormented existence. Thirsty enough to be drowned in his mercy and kindness. She wasn't the only one. Even me, I said my rosary every night before going to bed. Mother had just returned from hospital in Enugu where she got better diagnosis. The doctor said she would have died. She got a second chance and that's what her smile was for. A second chance. I watched her while leaning on the gmelina tree behind her, and tears streamed from my eyes. What if we had lost her. What if. I touched my tears and it's watery, and in my mouth, it's salty. We even shed the ocean when we cry. I smiled and cried seeing so much life in her. The sky was bright and tainted orange, clouds were moving underneath, forming swans and angles as they moved in the heavens. I washed my clothes in silence.

    Father slouched on an armchair by the hibiscus flower, sniffing tobacco. He never believed in anything. He never thought it was worth anything to believe. Not even the salvation of his own soul. He believed in going through life as it is and facing whatever that came to him. He was drowning under the weight of reality, too. It was all over his face. His eyes red shot with each sneeze. When the wind began to gain strength enough to shake his chair, he stood up and walked around the compound and looked at the fish pond behind the house and wondered if it was of any use, if it could provide the income that he needed the most. He once brought a man that looked at it and the man laughed and said it was better to build another one than to repair it. Yet, looking at it gave him a kind of hope I couldn't understand. Behind him was a cherry tree. I once saw a green snake eating cherries while playing Osadebe in the seating room. I did nothing but watch it slither from branch to branch. Father sighed and went to bed and I would stay up at night working on my school assignment with a lantern made of empty tin milk, filled with kerosene and a burning wick. The soot from it darkened the wall. I must have slept off at some point. I woke up in the middle of the night and saw father on the farm. I held the louver window and watched. There was dust on them, and I remembered it was my turn to clean them the next day. Father gathered firewood underneath the beehive and set them on fire. He ran back inside and went to bed. I watched the bees disperse in anger. Some wouldn't go far. They came back for their queen and died in the fire. The brave ones chose to die, and the cowards ran away, like in any other troubled colony ever established. In the morning, what remained was honey and honeycomb dropping into the bucket underneath.

 The boys hanging around the coconut trees were whispering about girls and when a girl walked past, they touched each other and encourage the one that was interested to go talk to her. John was among them. Tall, sly and knew his way around the street. A jolly good fellow. I can still hear his laughter echoing down the street. He walked with a slant to the right because almost everyone walked like that these days after watching hip-hop videos from America. Pitched coconut trees standing on a row right in front of the fence covered by green moss. John's dog kept on barking and wagging its tail by the boy's quarter apartment they rented out. John called me and gave me coconut's he harvested from their farm. I thanked him and dropped them on the wet sand. We sat down and talked about music. In the end, we concluded that Tupac drowned too because he couldn't go on living.

 In the beginning, God separated water from land. We only think so because that's all we can see. If you ask me, it is an illusion, and our street said so. It rained on Sunday and the water rose. The street was filled with so much water that we had to raise our clothes on our way to church. The water was all the way to our knees. Dressed in pristine traditional clothes, we sought the face of God. The priest talked about Noah and his boat. I wondered if it was going to happen to us because our street was already filled with water and the church compound too. Who would build the lords ark? I kept saying to myself while listening to a sermon.

At night, all the fireflies in the world gathered at the meadow and blinked. Tiny beautiful lights shining in the cover of darkness. I will lift up my eyes unto the hills, from whence cometh my help. My help cometh from the Lord, which made heaven and earth. We sat together as a family and read the word of God, and took turns to say what it meant to us. Torn blue upholstery, a new TV stand, an ironing table, and an old book shelf filled with books. We lay on the cold carpet listening to the word of God. But it wasn't all. There was news from Fatima. And the news from Fatima was prophesied in Umunya. Virgin Mary decided to visit Nigeria all the time, and through a virgin girl in Obowo, she announced a world with end.

"There will be three days of darkness. it will wipe away all evil from the earth. Only the righteous will survive. And like the Israelites, we will put a crucifix on our door front so that when the angels get to us, they will know we are Christians and pass. Judgment day is here and the angels will destroy everything that is evil," mother said. She always had that smile on her face even when she talked about apocalypse. She was seated on the blue upholstery torn in the middle.

"Will there be flood too?" I asked.

"No one knows," she said.

"What do we have to do to survive?" my sister asked.

"Prayer is the key. We must say the rosary all the time. Read the pamphlet too," mother said and gave us printed papers from the apparition ground and we read in silence and fear. There was a date all ready for it. The end of the millennium. From 31st December to the third of January. The year 2000 was only for the holy ones. We watched a movie afterward. It was the first VCR we bought. In the evening, I followed Mother to bury mustard seeds around the house as the prophetess instructed. We prayed and prayed and waited.

***

Water ran through the highway and into the smaller roads and unraveled all the memories of my childhood. It was very early in the morning and two boys stood under the coconut tree smoking weed. I was on my way to morning mass, to see redemption, ask for forgiveness of sin and ready for a world that was about to end. Did they know that the world was about to end? Did they know that smoking weed was a sin in the eyes of God and man because it made them do things they couldn't account for? Those that smoke weed were bound to be condemned. Halleluiah. Brother Mathew preached in St. Bridget's meeting, and the world darkened outside of the church. He said the lord was angry with sinners and asked us to pray for mercy upon the world, and we did.

Yahweh, do not be angry with us?

That morning, on my way back from church, I heard that one of the boys smoking weed went mad. Junior told me. He said he smoked something stronger than him. I can still picture his face. They called him Martin Cutest Fuckoyo. He was tall, pear-shaped head, and with an innocent face to go with it. Mother said we should pray for him, and father said that for once the bible was right. "The wages of sin is death," he mumbled while eating guava and seating near the hibiscus flower.

I sat on the cemented pavement and played Ludo with Junior.

"Do you guys know that the world is ending this year?" I asked him.

"No, who said that?" he asked, his eyes wide and brown. I knew he didn't know yet. I knew he wasn't catholic, but I wanted to bring the message to him too.

"In our church, a lady that the Virgin Mary speaks through said it."

"Well, it doesn't matter, does it? you Catholics always think that you know it all."

I knew he was going to say that. I knew he would bring the

denomination war again. Here, we fought on which side god was on. Mathew walked in holding a ball and news in his mouth. he wanted to play soccer with us.

"Do you know that they arrested the other boy that was smoking weed with Martin Cutest Fuckoyo?" Mathew said. None of us have heard that yet, and we were all surprised. I was expecting something like that too. I knew that Martin's mother wasn't going to take it lightly. I knew she would get the police involved. You only call the police for your worst enemy here. But having a son drown wasn't an easy thing to swallow.

***

on 31st night, we drew our curtains, bared the windows with wood and placed holly water on all corners of the house. We stayed inside praying and braced ourselves for the three days of darkness. Soon, it started raining. Mother said we shouldn't look outside. When we got tired praying, we drank holy water and ate a blessed biscuit. Father wasn't around. He stubbornly went to the village to see his mother. Mother prayed for him that he may be saved by the lord. I heard a sound outside, and I strongly believed that the angles were passing and must sight the crucifix on our door. We sang praises to the Lord for saving all of us in the room. We kept repeating the circle for three days. We couldn't tell if there was darkness outside because we bared the windows. On the third day, we opened our door and saw people walking up and down the street. We laughed and laughed and praised the Lord in any situation. It was funny indeed to think that only us would probably emerge from our street to behold the new day. I saw Junior passing by. I called him and he waved at me and said he was coming to play soccer later on. I was happy to see him. I was happy nothing really happened to people on our street apart from the water running to the mouth of the river. No matter what water did, I do not begrudge it.

James Reed

In the Presence of Ice

Emilio Bassoon brought his drawings from Europe in a flat box which resembled a tabletop despite its small handle padded with leather, as on the finest of luggage. Most Americans he'd met, in their bustling New World, were not accustomed to luxury. The more urban among them had fled impoverishment's close quarters, convinced that wide open spaces carried wealth on the winds, or at least in the soil. They had not encountered the splendors on view where business and commerce thrived in stone houses that rivaled cathedrals if not in their glory but unassailable presence. Every art, every industry, was put into play. People trapped in the warrens and hives and distemper of want were no more likely to witness magnificence than folks scattered in handfuls or dropped willy-nilly on a vast, empty continent ripe and ready for use.

Make no mistake. Emilio saw money. The plains appeared vacant, but cash was at hand, especially in unminted form, that wisp, opportunity. Chance was a factor, and fickle besides, but effort not made guaranteed failure. Attention employed was the first coin of investment.

Understanding that New York was fit for arrival but no nest for beginnings, Emilio rode trains farther westward in search of a spot where his worth might be noticed. Air not a hindrance to breath was important. Wood smoke, horse dung, and coal, while ubiquitous, he preferred not to find inescapable. Consumption he knew was slow, merciless terror. It shredded the lungs. All the while you spit blood.

His assortment of handkerchiefs grew by store and by town, however available. Should he someday be stricken he'd stand ready at once to give slight offence, to collect or conceal the droplets expelled. The cough was a struggle he'd heard far too often. It distressed all in earshot, whether well-known or strangers, and lately he counted as one of the latter.

To others, that is. To himself he was ordinary and therefore familiar. The one fixed point, though always in motion.

Not adrift, quite, but bereft of precision.

The idea seemed simple, at home, in his boredom, recognized now as no more than impatience. Foreign shores. Buy a ticket. Success and adventure surely awaited. In the meantime, however, he sat down to draw. Daily. Even now. Pen or pencil in hand allowed him to vanish. This was perfection. Infinite calm. Scratching and sketching to see what he knew.

Most days, very little.

"How's it you figure you're not wasting time?"

An unusual question. Most people, curious, admired the draughtsmanship. His machines put on paper were detailed and clean, even in their complexity. Each edifice, also, and the work less schematic, drew praise for the artistry. How like the tree, sky, or river, the fruit on the table, or the woman, so pensive, the noble fidelity to the truth of her soul, or his degradation, whatever viewers proclaimed. Personal embroidery, in the eyes of Emilio, with little bearing on the subjects as he meant them portrayed.

But this man, leaning close, half a foot from his shoulder and blocking his light, gazed at the flawless circles drawn freehand in one loop, a closed arc, without lifting the pencil, rondelles in an arch describing the entry to a structure not built or yet fully imagined. The man blinked at the parchment and the hotel over yonder, a clapboard affair with dusty, hazed windows and a horse tied out front, bridled, with no saddle, and unconcerned with its hind end while droppings fell steady.

Then stopped. The horse jerked its tail.

"It's quite a rendition, incomplete as it is, but since it's not there," the man waved a finger toward the horse and hotel, "I am prone to wonder why go to the trouble?"

"The pleasure." He put out his hand. "Emilio Bassoon."

"I see. Entertainment. It did not cross my mind." He studied the drawing. "I'm more fond of dalliance." He patted his trousers. "My personal worm." His fist clenched and opened. "Vim and vigor," he said. "It leads to vitality. Jonas Hancombe. Delighted. Welcome," he added.

"Welcome where?" asked Emilio. With an eye on the horse, he tugged loose a handkerchief.

"Unthank," said Hancombe. He poked his thumb backward toward the sign at the platform.

The block letters, squared off, he'd ignored. Noise for the eyes.

"Why Unthank?" he asked.

"Take a look."

The hotel needed paint. The horse started again. Emilio felt a tickle far back of his tongue.

"Do these people look grateful?" Hancombe guffawed.

The one soul on the street walked weighted down. The burlap bag slung on his shoulder was thick as a hog. It induced him to stagger.

"The dirt in these parts is dry as dead cats. The rain's done till fall unless it pours down big buckets. That'll wash clear away and take your house with it. These people are luckless and swear it's not so. Proof isn't good enough. They dig in blind as moles."

Plop-plop from the horse. "Unthank it is," Emilio said. His throat made a sound he hoped was genteel. He dabbed at his lips and, lifting the handkerchief, found it still dry.

"I save them," said Hancombe. "Give them a chance."

Emilio looked for a dowsing rod. The man travelled light. He carried a portable desk, probably mahogany, of the sort lieutenants and higher and, if they had them, their copyists utilized during campaigns. They dashed off dispatches, made out reports, composed letters and orders, and in sum gave account with pens and ink, sometimes pencils, on fine stock and stationery, kept in good order, with a stable, flat surface, all latched tight and convenient for quick use or storage as one wished or as needed.

The desk was in one hand, a small valise in the other. No forked stick or implement dangled in view. Emilio decided this was as expected. The man's shirt and jacket, his shoes and his trousers, showed signs of hard use, but all were expensive when originally purchased and well maintained since. The fellow took care, if for appearances only. He looked not designed to be digging in dirt for sparse water.

Except his hands, face, and hair were rough-hewn and windswept. Standing still with no breeze, he gave that impression. Bandy-legged and wiry, he was primed, energetic.

It was hot, here in Unthank. Both men dripped with sweat. "Save them how?" said Emilio. He could not imagine.

"I can't stop disasters or natural causes and don't claim so, either, but a few dollars now, in dribs over time, will ease the inevitable."

"Insurance," said Emilio.

"You're aware," Hancombe said. "I'd have guessed in a trice. You are a chap whose outlook is worldly."

A man with no pants, in a gingham shirt only, left the hotel. He stood by a barrel and spattered a while, staring hard at the sky, relieving himself.

Emilio watched, then shook his head.

"The sun shines every day upon wonders untold."

There wasn't a breeze or he'd smell the man's urine. The fellow leaned back as if pregnant, his output prodigious.

"Each man has a need. It can be quite specific. Ho-chunks and bohunks, I sell to them all. Take the time to explain, people see the advantage, if not for themselves, for their wives and their children. And sometimes their husbands. I find women canny."

The man finally stopped. The horse, though, continued. Neither seemed conscious at all of the other.

Emilio coughed, his mouth tightly closed.

"The trick is convince folks. Half think you're lying. The idea's unfamiliar. Indians especially lack background and know-how, but no man or woman can't tell when they're cheated. And their world's disappearing. Cash money and contracts are due to take over." Hancombe reached in a pocket. "Head Agent and Founder. I pay every claim. Word gets around. That's why I am trusted."

Emilio sounded out syllables he'd not seen or heard. "Og-la-la?"

"Like singing," laughed Hancombe," but no. Local people," he said. "In this empty country they're scattered and wandering and penned in and cornered. They're chasing a future. They got nothing else."

The card carried two emblems, a teepee on one side, depicted in triangles, with an elephant face opposite, the tusks curved toward circles and the head tall and tapered. Emilio, frankly, might have predicted a buffalo. Another creature he'd heard of was called an opossum.

Hancombe declared, "That's a fact shared in common. Them and us both, our breath's all we have. Oglala Life isn't just only Indians. Coloreds and Chinamen and us and whoever, we all need a leg up. Tomorrow is coming, sometimes today."

Emilio attempted to hand back the card. Hancombe said no.

"You may find it useful. Half my work's done. You knew the concept before we just met." He watched the waist-down naked man outside the hotel. "He himself has uncommon ambitions."

"Many do," said Emilio.

"He plants misshapen potatoes brought up from Peru."

The man spurted again and appeared to be startled. He hopped and bobbled to shake himself dry.

"They are vile and discolored, I am duly reminded. Like innards and viscera. Purple Poncas, he calls them." Hancombe stuck out his tongue and slashed a quick finger in front of his throat. "But he pays all his debts. He thinks he's entitled."

Emilio discovered his pencil had drifted. A faint line now straggled its way like a thread. He opened his box to retrieve an eraser.

"That is one excellent case. Hardwood?" said Hancombe. "May I ask where you bought it? Boston, perhaps?"

"A man from Bavaria. He built it and shipped it. He passed through on a pilgrimage to admire cathedrals. He carved saints and angels."

"Was his interest in history or ahead, the Hereafter?"

"Carpentry," said Emilio. "Charging a fee."

Curiosity slowly gave way to a grin. "You're acquainted with commerce."

Hancombe seemed cheered by a notion Emilio found merely straightforward. Here was a man who hungered for money.

Emilio secured the compartment holding erasers, small brushes, and other aids toward correction but gave Hancombe time to take notice of brass rules and compasses, protractors, devices exacting and various, held in place by snug ribbons or straps of trim leather. "The instruments are English." He latched the box closed.

"Your profession," said Hancombe, "as well as amusement."

Gum eraser in hand, Emilio permitted a hint of a smile and swept crumbs from the vellum with a brush of black horse hair.

Across the street there were loud snuffles and whinnies. The man with no pants might have lost footing. His bare legs thrashed and spraddled as he clung to the neck of the horse, which now panicked. It reared back and kicked, but in fear, like small dogs, it was voiding its pizzle. The noise and the splashing and smell were horrendous. Emilio's throat clenched and scraped ragged. His very lungs he thought pockmarked, as if pitted with cinders.

"The man, to his credit, carries a policy against total crop failure and pays up on time. He's not once filed a claim. The ugly spuds are successful. He does not shirk, thieve, or lie. Such clients in abundance would do me great good."

Emilio coughed, felt his handkerchief moisten. He balled it up in a pocket to boil once with strong soap and steep later with lavender, although in this country he'd run across sage. Some thought it medicinal. Crushed, smoked, or simmered, it emboldened the air and enhanced inhalation.

He retrieved a new handkerchief and mopped at his brow. His sweat wasn't fever but the heat of this place. Good news, he decided. He wasn't yet ill.

The man regained his posture and tugged at his shirttail as if to be tidy if not quite presentable. He scratched at his belly and lifted each foot to shake loose the dust or stray insects and yawped as he yawned, both arms outstretched as if he meant to encompass the great dome of the heavens.

Or sneeze. Loudly, in fact. The horse shook its head.

The man sneezed again and swiped a sleeve under his nose. He pressed his palms to his eyeballs and yawned less rambunctiously. His lips smack as if finding a new taste on his tongue, hands smoothing the gingham like a comfortable nightshirt.

He trudged back inside, and Jonas Hancombe yawned also. "I can't sleep for spit. I lie down for hours half-awake dead and finally get up to make use of my time. It's not fair you should die. Putrefaction's the swindle. That process will stop in the presence of ice."

Emilio remembered great blocks chopped from lakes and hauled swaddled in sawdust. It melted in huts, but with such calm and so slowly it might last a whole year.

"Endless winter in Russia has this frostbitten soil. It never does thaw or turn solid, either. In the ground there they've found these big, hairy elephants, with long fur like switchgrass as red as the pelt on the head of your average Glass Weedgin."

Emilio blinked.

"Scotsman," said Hancombe. "Bagpipes and kilts. Think of it, though. Red-haired giant elephants, alive as the two of us. Dead now for centuries in frozen dirt but still they look good. They could wake up tomorrow and scare hell out of bison. I say that because they're also here, too. An old Lakota man told me. Up north, down in caves. The air's chilled because there's this ice never melts."

"I could stand not to sweat," Emilio mentioned.

"They lie there like sleeping, these thick-haired monster elephants, not wrinkled gray wrecks like you see in the circus. You'd swear good and ready to get up and walk." He set down his desk and valise and pulled a flask from a pocket. "I need a sip. Join me?" he said.

Emilio declined.

"Smart man." Hancombe gulped once and shuddered. "Rigor snortis," he said. "Keeps a man limber." He screwed on the cap. "Boy, I sure hope so. I don't want to die. I dream about that. Herds of red elephants wake up underground and shake ice off their fur." He slipped the flask in his pocket. "Except I can't sleep. Hardly. Not much. I got too much to do."

A squared-cornered funnel shape appeared on the vellum, the cone top like a tulip, the tube a dense stack. Red brick. Ochre. Older than iron.

Hancombe put his eyes close, inches out from Emilio's. "You look pretty rested. Your sleep any good?"

"I awaken to footsteps. No one is found."

"Your whole life," Hancombe asked, "or one place and no other?"

"Always. Forever. In this country, too."

"You got ghosts," Hancombe said. "They follow you around. They're probably waiting."

Out of sight, thought Emilio. That much was a courtesy.

His pencil found purchase. For Hancombe, from memory, Emilio summoned the tower from home, thickset and massive, with pooled air enclosed by walls tall and mighty as ancient red elephants. Perhaps he might sleep. Perhaps he'd find solace.

The horse lifted its tail, unconcerned as a cow.

Emilio cleared the scratch in his throat, a fresh handkerchief still folded, pressed close as a bandage to cover his mouth.

Thorns & Roses, a baseball poem

Rose bush – being there –
all my growing
thorns & roses life
as each ancestor passed
by it, where all of us
as children played, built
snow mountain beside it
& summers' blooms listened
when all elders alive then
sat on the porch tuned-in
to the Phillies radio station.
Announcer calling each
swing and a miss, each pitch,
runs batted in. As if ancestral
wisdom passed down in 9
innings: balls & bats
diamonds & dugouts
jeers & cheers; wins & loses;
safe & out. So many lives
passed by & in passing on
to another place, each hearse
driven coffin's last drive-by
home plate & rose garden,
before their body's final
disappearance into sacred.
Now, the very last relative
& house, retired. So today,
after reshaping thorns & roses
for winter like a groundskeeper,
I clean up clippings, hand
ruby love to her from my glove
& take one home with me.
Place thorn cut stem & last full bloom
into Phillies beer glass of tap
water on kitchen's windowsill.
Elbows deep in snowy mound
of soapy suds, look

into rose's anonymous pupil
surrounded by petals of ruby
slippers tapping together touch
whispering each ancestors'
faded name, home & safe.

Diane Sahms

Coming and Going

I didn't know I had a roommate
until I caught her in the spare bedroom
packing her bags. "Some days,"
she said, "you act like you don't know
I am alive." She was wearing a peach
colored top, white fringe on
the sweetheart neckline. The teardrops
looked like olive juice stains on her breast.

Steve Sibra

In Between

I am surrounded by
Life's astounding beauty:

the smell of jasmine on crystal nights,
a newborn's steady gaze,
waves crashing onto craggy shores.

I am surrounded by
Life's enormous pain:
a kitten, flattened leather between the tracks,
The stench and stain of dementia,
Men shivering on sidewalks.

I spend most of my time in that divide,
dull as a beige wall, tired as mud.

Jeri Thompson

Like Heaven Itself

Jesus is coming back,
but it's not going to be
maybe what you expect.
No, no ticker-tape parades,
or football stadium sermons.
No concert tours with Bob Dylan,
and not a single meeting with the Pope,
nor even any isolated encounters
with Mexican peasant women.

No, in fact, he won't be here long.
The rumor is just one Saturday,
probably next October He's going
to sign stuff and pose for photos
with fans like old baseball players do
at that big outlet mall north of Pittsburgh.
They say he needs some quick cash;
the taxes on his condo in heaven
have skyrocketed and the cost
of his prescription meds coupled
with the hip replacement surgery,
has gone through the roof.

So, look around in the basement
or attic for your family Bible,
and plan to get there early.
You can bet parking is going
to be a real bitch and the line
to see him like heaven itself,
full of assholes, long as forever,
and boring as hell.

David J. Thompson

The Voice of Fred Flintstone

For weeks before his audition
we heard my dad rehearsing
to be the voice of Fred Flintstone.
Our hopes were sky high,
but when he got the phone call
that said he didn't get the role,
we knew what was coming.
He drank half a bottle of Jim Beam
with Budweiser chasers
at the kitchen table, muttering
about how he'd show them
what a real caveman was.
Suddenly, he slapped the table
hard with the palm of his hand,
stood up, and grabbed me by the arm
and my sister by her hair,
locked us in the hall closet.
My mom was screaming,
No, no! and there in the dark
we heard him slapping, then
knocking her down. We'd seen
all this before, too many times.

Luckily, some weary neighbors called
the cops; we heard the siren before
any bones were broken. The three of us
stood on the front porch as they led
my handcuffed dad down to the prowl car.
Yabba dabba doo, I heard my mom say
under her breath while holding a dish towel
full of ice to the other side of her face.
Yabba dabba fucking doo.

David J. Thompson

Kareem Tayyar

The Road to Los Angeles

My wife had always hated me picking up hitchhikers. She was one of those true-crime fanatics, the kind who devoured paperbacks with titles like *My Brother Was a Serial Killer* and *Our Next Door Neighbor Murdered the Black Dahlia*, and whom, when she wasn't reading, would watch the nightly news and nod her head at the latest travesty out of Lebanon or Ethiopia or East St. Louis and say, "You see what I mean? It's all gone to hell," and then, when I would try to lift her spirits by telling her that the Dodgers had taken four from the Giants or that a trio of baby Chinese pandas were going to be at the zoo all summer, she'd smile, playfully wag her finger at me and say, "I see what you're trying to do. It won't work." But I guess none of that – not the hitchhikers, nor the murderous neighbors, nor the civil war in Beirut – was my problem any more. Katherine and I had been separated for five months, and hadn't spoken in three.

Which was why, less than ten minutes outside of Albuquerque, and on my way back from a three-day shoot on the set of some second-rate action film whose star was such a diva that he'd demanded a stunt double for otherwise routine horse-riding scenes, I pulled to the shoulder of Interstate 40, rolled down my window, and told the guy with a small cardboard sign that read *Winslow Bound* to hop in.

Four hours later, and after an extended monologue of his that covered everything from his belief that John Wayne was the living reincarnation of John Wilkes Booth, to his certainty that it was the Mormons who'd been responsible for the coverup at Area 51, to his recently discovered finding that Shoeless Joe Jackson had helped fix the 1919 World Series on behalf of Czarist Russia, I'd dropped the man, whose name I never learned, a few miles from Monument Valley, in front of a trailer parked in an otherwise vacant lot populated by waist-high weeds and more prairie dogs than I could count. He said it belonged to his girl, whom he hadn't seen since the previous summer, when the two of them had parted ways with some particularly harsh words after a night of dropping acid at CBGB that featured a headlining set by the Ramones. I wished him luck. He said only Birchers and anarchists believed in luck; instead he pulled a turquoise opal in the shape of an elephant from his pocket, handed it to me, and said,

"Always make sure the trunk points towards the window."

He was out the door and heading towards the house before I could thank him. And he didn't look back, not even before, without knocking, he'd entered and disappeared inside.

It was just before I'd left the Phoenix city limits that I spotted another one, this time a young woman – girl, really – fifteen or sixteen, whose heavy red backpack made it look like she was preparing to climb Kilimanjaro, and whose long hair, sandy blonde, gave her the look of a hippie too young to know that that particular circus had long ago packed up and left town.

She hesitated for a few beats when I'd pulled over, as she looked through my window and tried to gauge whether I was someone she could trust. Having apparently decided that highway marauders didn't usually drive beat-up Trans Ams and feature scars that ran from just above their jawlines to an inch or so beneath their right cheekbones – it would have been too obvious, the kind of cliché that one only saw in the type of Hollywood pictures that I so often doubled in – she opened the door, slid in and, after throwing her bag in the back, studied my face for another few seconds, a face which included the beginnings of gray in the temples and a tan so permanent that a winter in Antarctica wouldn't have done anything to lessen its darkness, and said,

"You get that scar in Vietnam?"

"Not exactly," I said, hitting the accelerator and merging back onto Interstate 93.

"What does that mean?"

"It means I got it on a backlot off Sunset that had been made to look like Vietnam."

"I don't get it."

"I was doing stunt work on some picture about a young kid who goes to Vietnam thinking it's going to be the Green Berets, you know?, hanging from helicopters and picking off VC with an automatic weapon in each hand, who then realizes that the whole thing is Hell on Earth and that LBJ was as full of shit as Rusk and McNamara and the rest of the so-called 'Best and Brightest' had been."

I glanced at her to see if she was listening; it was clear that she expected me to keep going.

"So anyway," I continued, noticing that, even though it was nearly evening, one could still see what appeared to be an eternally shimmering oasis a few hundred yards further up the highway, "I'm supposed to jump off the back of this jeep that's moving at top speed, somersault, and then rise up, pull the pin on the grenade I've got in my hand, and throw it over a set of sandbags that the enemy is holed up behind."

"And?" she asked, as she sipped from a thermos she'd affixed with a peace sign sticker.

"And I did," I said. "But the driver swerved right when he was supposed to swerve left, so I didn't make the leap as cleanly as I would have liked. The ground made sure I paid for that mistake."

She held the thermos out to me; I shook my head.

"That's a hell of a silly way to punch up your face."

"Don't I know it? I'm Frank, by the way."

"Dorothy."

"Like *The Wizard of Oz*."

"I've never seen it."

"That doesn't seem possible."

She shrugged her shoulders.

"How far are you going, Frank?"

"Los Angeles."

"Perfect," she said.

For the next hour we didn't speak. Instead we moved in silence through a desert landscape heavy on boarded-up motels, roadside crucifixes, and billboards alerting us to the fact that a McDonalds, or a Motel 6, or an Exxon, was always only a few miles further on ahead. Halfway through this silence Dorothy reached over and turned on the radio with the kind of casual comfort with which a teenaged daughter, bored by her father's inability to maintain a conversation, decided that a soundtrack was necessary to see her through the monotony.

A few seconds later, after a quick run through the dial, she settled on a famous tune from the early 1970s, where John Fogerty sings about a run through the jungle that, from the tone of his voice, you knew had no chance of ending well.

Twilight, then dusk, then darkness.

"You don't say much, do you?" she asked, as the Rolling Stones came on the radio, Mick Jagger wailing in a cheap falsetto about the woman he missed.

"I'm just trying to figure out what a girl your age is doing on the road."

"On the road?" she laughed, and put her feet on the dashboard. "You make it sound like I'm Kerouac or something. But it's nothing special. I'm going to see someone in L.A."

"Yeah? What someone?"

"My mother."

I reached over to turn down the volume on the radio. It wasn't a full moon, but it was close enough. And there were more stars in the sky than I'd seen in L.A. during the previous year combined.

"How long's it been since you've seen her?"

"I've never seen her," she said, turning her head to look out the passenger-side window, suddenly seeming less like a teenager desperately trying to pass for an adult and more like a teenager doing everything she could not to reveal the little girl she still secretly felt herself to be. "At least not that I can remember."

Splashes of orange, red. One silhouette moving, a second one seeming to recline like some kind of moonlit odalisque across the pavement.

"Don't look," I said, slowing the car.

She crossed her arms tightly to her chest and stared through the windshield at the small fire that burned from the overturned vehicle's hood.

I pulled to the shoulder.

"Stay here," I said.

She didn't nod, or respond in any way, other than to keep her eyes fixed on mine with an intensity that made me feel as if I were committing an unforgivable sin simply by leaving her alone for a matter of moments.

It was, or had been, at least, a Mercedes S class. Probably a '78 or '79, with the type of chrome hubcaps that gave the illusion they were spinning backwards while the car was in motion. Two remained on the wheels; the third lay like a miniature flying saucer a few feet from the wreck, and the fourth rolled slowly into the distance, like those animals one hears about whose legs keep moving for several seconds after their heads have been separated from their bodies.

The moving silhouette was a man a few years older than me. Thirty-eight, maybe thirty-nine. In his right hand he was holding his car keys; in his left he was holding what, upon closer inspection, was revealed to be a significant portion of the tongue of his passenger, a woman the bottom half of whose body remained in the car, and whose top half protruded from the shattered passenger-side window.

"They grow back, I think?" the man asked in his shock. "Right?" he insisted, as he approached me, his hand holding out the tongue as a kind of offering, a communion wafer pilfered from the land of the dead.

I closed his hand around the tongue, and led the man towards the grass beside the shoulder.

"You," he said with surprise, as a bit of blood began to inch from his ear.

I followed his eyes to where they had fixed on Dorothy, who stood several feet from us, her arms still crossed at her chest in a vain attempt to warm herself from a night whose temperature had dropped quickly.

"Go back to the car," I said.

"*You*," he said again, this time with a softness in his voice that seemed to articulate relief. He sat down in the grass. Dorothy remained where she was.

I took her by the arm, and pointed towards the white-and-blue Chevron sign that shone like a low-hanging constellation just off the highway.

"You see that? It's going to be about a quarter-mile's walk from here," I said. "Use the cashier's phone to call for help. We're on Route 93, a few clicks past the River Street exit."

"Clicks?" she said, her eyes widening. "I thought you said you weren't in Vietnam."

"I said I didn't get that scar in Vietnam. Now go."

"My bag," she said, in such a way that made me worry that if she remained at the scene for any longer, she herself might slip into shock.

"It's safe," I said. "I'll pick you up there once the police have arrived. Go. Now. Sweetheart.," I said, a word I don't believe I'd ever used in my life, but one my own mother had used often me with me when I was a boy.

Once she'd gone I moved back to the woman in the automobile and checked for a pulse I knew I wouldn't find. Blond, with red lipstick carefully applied, and red nails with little white hearts painted onto the index fingers of each one, she was the type of woman who got dressed up for something as simple as a trip to the grocery store. I removed my jacket and draped it over her the same way the nurses had when our only child, a boy my wife and I had agreed to name Timothy, had arrived stillborn.

It was a few seconds later that I saw the elk. Lying on his side, its lifeless eyes opened and looking up at a moon it was probably seeing for the very first time.

I turned back towards the shoulder to see the man no longer visible in the grass. Upon approaching, I found him lying on his side, his keys catching the moonlight just enough to illuminate the almost beatific look he had on his face.

Only a single car passed in the hour before the first authority arrived – a haggard sixty-something sheriff with a small gut and a large gun and an indifferent look on his face that made me hate him instantly – and, upon slowing down and registering the scene of carnage, sped off, rather than stopping to see if there was anything its occupants could do. Of course there wasn't. Which didn't make their refusal to stop any more unforgivable.

In short order another sheriff's vehicle arrived on the scene, along with two ambulances, a fire truck, a tow truck, and a highway patrolwoman who barely looked older than Dorothy but who carried herself with a gravitas which none of the men, not even had they been fortunate to have lived for another several centuries, could have ever begun to approach.

It was she who took my statement, and who asked what, if anything, I had seen upon arriving.

"How did you call it in?"

"I didn't," I said, and then explained about Dorothy.

"She's your daughter?"

"No," I said, and was surprised to find a twinge at my response that made me wish as if my answer had been otherwise. "But I'm taking her to see her mother."

"This is the third one of these we've had this month," she said, gazing back in the direction of the accident, where the tow truck's crane had, as if it were the hand of an indifferent god, reached down from its elevated height and latched onto the crushed hood of the automobile. The entire scene reminded me of an art installation imagined by some homicidal Rauschenberg, a Warhol with a mean streak. "The stars aren't enough to illuminate the road, and by the time the driver awakens from his half-sleep to realize there's an elk or a deer or, in the case of the one last week, a bison, right in front of him, it's too late for the driver to do anything but wish he'd been more of a religious man than he was."

The drive to retrieve Dorothy from the Chevron station took less than ten minutes, but it was enough. Enough to send me nearly a decade back into the past, where a scared, younger version of myself parachuted out of airplanes and floated to earth hoping that his endless repetitions of the Our Father would be sufficient armor to keep him from being shot out of the sky. Enough to see the faces of Wildcat, Blue Hector, and the Big Tennessee, none of them twenty years old, none of them men I would ever again have the opportunity to meet in this world.

Enough, also, to think about all the ways in which one's life is less a matter of decisions made and roads not taken than it is a series of chapters in a book by an author who believes neither in plot nor in resolution. We enter scenes unaware of the roles we are meant to play, the people we are meant to interact with, the opportunities and obstacles that we are about to confront. Through a glass darkly? Please. I'd love to know what St. Paul would have had to say after ten months in Saigon, or whether, after a decade back home, the writer of First Corinthians would have still believed in divine fate when it was all he could do not to break the water glass on his teeth every night.

Dorothy was sitting on the curb in front of the gas station, drinking from a can of Coca-Cola, when I arrived. To her right a semi-truck was parked beside one of the pumps, and its driver leaned against the trailer smoking a cigarette. The moon had vanished behind a thicket of clouds, and the cold continued to intensify. It had still been autumn when the day began; it was autumn no longer.

I put the car in neutral, stepped out, and walked around to where she sat.

"You did good."

"Is the man ok?"

"He's fine," I lied. "On his way to the hospital as we speak."

"What about the animal?"

I shook my head.

It was clear she had something else she wanted to say; I didn't rush her.

"I almost rode with them," she said, lifting her head to look at me. "Earlier. They had pulled over about ten or fifteen minutes before you did. They were on their way to Los Angeles too."

She was fighting one hell of a battle with her tear-ducts, and so far at least, she seemed to be winning. Her hands and forearms, however, shook like those of an aging prizefighter who had taken too many shots to the head. I sat next to her on the curb, accepted the can from her hands, and took a long drink.

"Why didn't you get in?" I asked, handing the can back to her.

"It's stupid," she said, looking down.

"How so?"

"I didn't want to ride in a foreign car."

"What?"

"My dad spent the past seven years working at the Ford plant in Gallup. Transmissions, mostly. But he'd done it all, at one time or another. Wheels, hoods, steering columns. Anyway they laid him off last month. Everyone, actually. The whole operation is moving to Mexico. It's cheaper, I guess."

Behind us the cashier turned out the lights to the station. The truck pulled away from the pump and lumbered back out onto the road. Dorothy continued.

"It just felt disloyal not to drive American."

I laughed softly; I couldn't help it.

"Well, your economic patriotism just saved your life."

She said something under her breath that I couldn't hear.

"What was that?" I asked.

"He's dead, isn't he?" she repeated.

"Yes," I said, then, taking her by the arm, helped her to stand. "Come on. We'll find a place to stay for the night and get to L.A. in the morning.

We checked out of the motel at 10 a.m. the next day. It was later than I'd planned on leaving, but Dorothy had slept so soundly that it would have been a crime to wake her any earlier. Once we got situated in the car, she fell immediately back to sleep and didn't awaken until we'd hit Riverside, which, as always, smelled like cow-shit and looked like Alabama without the Confederate flags.

"Are we there?" she asked, rubbing her eyes.

"Soon," I said.

She took a few more minutes to fully awaken, and then reached over the seat to grab her backpack. I'd had the radio low while she slept. At the moment it was playing something off the new Springsteen album. There were few things in those years that sounded better than Clarence Clemons' saxophone.

"Your mother know you're coming?" I asked.

She took her time in answering, instead focusing on locating a half sheet of paper from one of the many pockets of her backpack.

"Not exactly," she said, unfolding the paper and studying what was written on it.

"How's that?"

She refolded the paper, looked out at yet another stretch of abandoned houses, rusting tractors, and men picking strawberries for less than two dollars an hour and said,

"My mother is dead."

Even with all these many decades now passed, that moment still reminds me that whatever it is that we have suffered in our lives, whatever disappointments and setbacks, heartbreaks and missed opportunities, there is always someone, usually close enough for us to touch, that has endured far worse. Not that this is any great philosophical revelation or anything; still, there are times we are reminded of it with such unexpected force that it's all we can do to keep our eyes on the road and our hands on the wheel.

I'd like to think I responded quickly to what she said, therefore providing her with, however inadequate to the enormity of her circumstances, at least some sense that she wasn't as alone in the universe as she must have felt at that moment, but the truth is I'm almost certain I let the song play out, and the next one begin, before I finally spoke.

"Where are you planning to stay?"

Again the shoulder shrug, followed by her looking down at her palms, as if she were attempting to read her own fortune.

"I'll think of something."

"You want to tell me what happened to her?"

The van in front of us featured one of those full-sized murals that were popular in those days: there was a blue ocean out of which a mermaid rose from the water with a trident in her right hand and her head turned towards the sky, as if the sea-goddess were ready to take on whatever the heavens threw at her. At any other moment I would have thought it the silliest thing I'd ever seen; but for whatever reason, at that moment it had inspired in me a desire to cry that I had to fight with everything I possessed not to give into.

"Same thing as you," she said. "Although not exactly, I guess."

"I don't follow."

"She got sent to Vietnam, and then she didn't come back."

The van ahead of us took the next off-ramp. To our left a large cross had been affixed atop one of the hills. I've never understood our desire to plant crosses or flags wherever we can. Some nights I still dream of being an astronaut just so I can remove the one they'd placed on the surface of the moon all those years ago.

"Women didn't get sent to Vietnam."

"Mine did," she said. "She was a nurse in a hospital in Santa Fe. And when her brother got killed over there, she figured it was her duty to take his place. She was in country for seven months, and then one afternoon the plane she was riding in, along with thirty-seven Vietnamese kids and a handful of other nurses and I think one or two soldiers, got shot out of the sky. Or maybe the engines just failed. I don't know. All that matters is the plane went down, and nobody survived."

"There couldn't have been more than a handful of American women who died over there."

"Nine," she said, with authority, and then proceeded to list, in alphabetical order, each of their names, along with the specific dates of their deaths and the names of the family members they were survived by.

Once she'd finished, I nodded down at the slip of paper she clutched the way a particularly pious nun might grip a rosary, and asked,

"What's on the paper?"

"The cemetery address."

"Is she at the one off Wilshire? Los Angeles National?"

"You know it?" she asked, her voice having slipped into a register higher than her normal one in relief that she was no longer, at least not entirely, heading into unfamiliar territory.

It was hard to miss. Even by 1980 the City of Angels had lost enough men to two World Wars, Korea, Vietnam, and a host of other smaller conflicts to require a cemetery large enough to have earned its own area code. Whenever I'd driven past it during my years in L.A. there were so many white crosses that it sometimes seemed as if they might track you all the way to the sea.

"I'll take you," I said.

"You don't have to do that."

"Yeah? Alright, I'll just drop you off here so I can make my 1 o'clock tee time."

It was the first time I'd heard her laugh since I'd picked her up.

"Guys like you don't golf, Frank."

"It's that obvious?"

"Yes," she said, and then started to cry.

It was a little after three p.m. by the time we arrived, and it was closer to four by the time we'd located, with the help of the kindly soldier who'd been stationed at the front desk, the precise location of Jennifer Abbey Washington's – First Lieutenant, United States Army – gravesite.

"I forgot to bring flowers", Dorothy said to me as we approached. The cross was in one of the newer sections of the cemetery, which featured a trio of large oak trees that provided around-the-clock shade.

"She isn't going to mind," I said. "She'll just be happy to see you."

"What should I say?" she asked, as in the street just beyond the cemetery fence a couple of young girls roller-skated in the direction of an ice cream truck that had just turned the corner.

"Whatever you want," I said. "Or nothing at all. You'll figure it out."

I remained where I was, standing in the small, paved lane where we'd parked the car, leaning against the door of the Trans Am. I thought about the day I'd shipped home, landing at Pendleton, to find that my mother and father were both there to greet me; I thought about those moments of elation Katherine and I had felt when we'd first learned she was pregnant; I thought about the joys of riding a horse on flat ground in the direction of the setting sun, whether or not a camera was running. I thought about fathers and daughters; about husbands and wives; about all the ways the country we love breaks us; and about the rare people we come across who put us back together.

Afterwards we had an early dinner at an old diner at the far end of the Miracle Mile. I called Katherine from a pay phone at the back, and we waited for her to arrive before we ordered.

In she, sank

my body bag – exactly
as it has never been
described – because I've
wharved & dipped in
postures to be known for

*(in an alone wind the swan's song massaging we are
our own trees falling a crescent cemetery with the stillness
of a placid pond longing who ironed cool biles
with so many visits)*

In she, sank

Feigned fruit
This folding soul
In shy rivalry

Speak
Thine
Sea
Unto

Beddings   of notions
Fingering across   my

Whistling into
The dark – wending
Holy your foul anchor

Kristin Withers

Invasive

Then there was no more singing.
All the lights in their throats cut:

the protest of evening wolves & black
bears nuzzling a parched creek for any-

thing that might sustain them another
white-skinned winter, those foreign

birds we never learned the names for.
Invasive, my grandfather called them.

Like the silver carp haunting our
local river. Bullfrogs & possums.

He called us *natives* after living
three generations on the same

hard land it took so much blood
to own. At the end of the path

the bullet takes to meet the right
body, the right body drops like

nothing worth losing sleep over.
It'll cost two men three hours

to drag it home in one piece.
That wilder silence lasts but

a brief eternity. Before the unseen
choir shakes the forest. Again,

the same damn wolves & starlings. Men
still dragging. The season closing.

Its wiry legs kick & quiver in our hands.
Like strings. Song. Our song now to sing.

John Sibley Williams

Yes, Rev. Father, I am Dead

We are writing to know if it is true that you are DEAD.
    – e-mail from Rev. Father Austine Dike, Nigeria

News of my DEATH "brought great shock" to your minds?
    Think what it did to mine, coming just as I was poised
to claim my "US $5.5M," quit my job as First Taster
    at Glendale Water Reclamation, and marry Carrie Underwood.

(If I'd gown up with less meth and more girls like her, I might
    have died with my own teeth.) I'd planned to call
on Carrie in my coonskin cap, then, after a bit of backwoods
    chat, throw down the cap, shuck off my dungarees,

and stand revealed, in new Armani duds, as the stud
    $5.5M would've made me. Thus decompose the best-
laid plans. By the way, heaven isn't as you Rev. Fathers
    preach. The streets are paved with Egg McMuffins –

not great, especially after Jesus strolls by with his sheep.
    No one sees God. He's "in a meeting" if you call –
Lord knows with whom; but St. Peter won't say. The angels
    are winged turtles who musk your face and flap away.

The IRS has agents here; but there's no Internet, or even a post
    office to slog my "SS number" to you "within three
working days." Or ever. You can never be certain
    I am DEAD. (This, let me state, is strange to be.

One instant, your cells seethe with energy; the next,
    all those mitochondrial power-plants shut down.
One instant, electricity is ziggling through more neurons
    than Andromeda has stars; the next, it all just sniggles out).

Best keep my cash safe, Rev. Dad. For all you know,
    I'll show up, packing. Picture yourself on that day,
looking guilty, feeling worse. Fear of that is what I send you –
    and, for hoping I'm an idiot, this curse.

Charles Harper Webb

reviewed by Jonah Raskin

Beat Scrapbook by Gerald Nicosia

Coolgrove Press, 2020, 130 pp., paper

Gerald Nicosia loves the writers of the Beat Generation. He has always loved them, beginning in his boyhood and continuing all the way to northern California where he lives today and writes up a storm. The author of *Memory Babe*, a big and comprehensive, though "critical biography" of the author of *On the Road,* Nicosia is also a fierce poet who carries on the legacy of the Beats who altered the course of American verse in the 1940s.

Nicosia's love and admiration for them and their work shine brightly in *Beat Scrapbook (Coolgrove Press),* his new book that packs a wallop and pays homage to Jack Kerouac and his daughter Jan, Lawrence Ferlinghetti, William Burroughs, Lenore Kandel, Charles Bukowski, Richard Brautigan, Gregory Corso and more. Indeed, the gang's all here.

There's also a longish love poem to "The Beauties of My Generation" that comes with four-letter words and that extols the "naked-rainbow-hued young bodies on the streets of San Francisco." The city by the bay is a kind of "secret hero" in *Beat Scrapbook*. ("Secret Hero" is the phrase that Ginsberg uses in *Howl* to describe Neal Cassady.) Nicosia goes back and forth from Chicago, "his hometown," to the city that he has adopted as his own and with detours to Lowell, Massachusetts, Kerouac's birthplace and stomping ground. In "The Ghost of Kerouac," Nicosia sets the stage for his reveries with the past, describing the "teenage school kids" hurrying home, perhaps with copies of *The Dharma Bums* under their arms. Nicosia imagines himself walking with the ghost of Lowell's world famous author. What a lovely idea!

About that irascible Beat poet, Jack Micheline – whose full name was Harvey Martin Silver Jack Micheline – Nicosia writes, "You didn't take shit from no one" and "yet you were full of love too." There's a certain amount of sentimentality in these pages – a yearning for a lost time and place – but there are also humorous anecdotes, as when Nicosia describes the time he showed up at City Lights to interview Ferlinghetti and Ferlinghetti told him, "You need a better microphone than that."

Kerouac might be a ghost in *Beat Scrapbook*, but he's a palpable ghost. One feels his presence and the presence of his buddies in this book. Nicosia doesn't just write about the famous Beats. He also takes time to depict lesser known figures like David Meltzer, a brilliant performer on stage, in a poem titled "The Poet as Proteus." Like the best Kerouac poems, Nicosia's poems have rhythm. You can practically hear his voice and hear a saxophone in the background. If you have trouble getting his rhythms, you might try reading the poems out loud.

Michael Schumacher, the author of *Dharma Lion*, a magnificent biography of Allen Ginsberg, provides a stunning introduction in which he writes that "poets, it seems to me, are tellers of secrets." Schumacher adds that "reading Nicosia's poetic scrapbook, you feel as if you are at a parade, standing curbside, watching familiar faces walk by." Nicosia makes the familiar seem new and the new seem familiar.

If Schumacher's introduction doesn't persuade you to read Nicosia's book, perhaps the first few poems themselves will entice you, as when he writes "There are deer and there are hawks but there/ Is only one Gary Snyder." Linking Snyder to wild animals is the perfect way to introduce him.

There is also only one Gerald Nicosia, a poet with brothers and sisters galore who isn't afraid to show his own beating heart and his unabashed love for a generation of writers and for "angel headed hipsters" who woke America from its romance with the Bomb, with war and with material things, and injected honest-to-goodness spirituality into the life of the nation itself.

reviewed by Ron McFarland

Making Landfall by Paul Lindholdt

Encircle Publications, Farmington, ME, 2018, 81 pp., $15.99

Consider this alternative definition of the acronym IPO so familiar to those who follow the world of high finance: Initial Poetic Offer – the poem that opens any given collection.

Why do poets decide to open their books the way they do? Surely, I've long presumed, they must assume the potential buyer of their book will read the opening poem and quite plausibly decide, sensibly or not, whether to pursue the matter any further. If my premise is correct, quite a lot depends on that opening poem. Reaching back to the Renaissance, poets commonly offered up a prefatory verse, "To the Reader," or perhaps "To the Gentle Reader." Charles Baudelaire's *Les Fleurs du mal* (1857) opens notoriously with "Au Lecteur," something of an anti-dedication in which he lashes out at the reader as a fellow hypocrite prey to that worst of monsters, ennui. Billy Collins playfully (of course!) dabbles in mock dedications at times, mentioning Baudelaire in the first line of "Dear Reader" in *The Art of Drowning* (1995) and opening *Picnic, Lightning* (1998) with "A Portrait of the Reader with a Bowl of Cereal." Readers who take up Baudelaire's or Collins's books based on their positive reception of the supposed dedicatory poems will be neither surprised nor disappointed. In a similar vein, W.S. Merwin begins *Travels* (1993) in Baudelairean fashion with "Cover Note": "Hypocrite reader my / variant my almost / family," lamenting the decline in the readership for poems and his lack of "the ancients' confidence" that posterity will understand "our true meaning."

Viewed from the perspective of 20/20 hindsight, some poets have begun their books with what now appear to have been prophetic decisions, selecting poems that would be oft anthologized in years to come. Robert Frost introduced readers of *North of Boston* (1915), his second book, with the eight-liner, "The Pasture," which surely comes across as an invitation: "I'm going out to clean the pasture spring," the two-quatrain poem begins, and each of the quatrains ends, "I shan't be gone long – You come too." The initial poem of what one might consider the body of the text is "The Mending Wall," with its refrain, "Good fences make good neighbors." The next year he opened *Mountain Interval* with "The Road Not Taken." His 1924 Pulitzer Prize-winning collection, *New Hampshire*, begins with the rather long title poem, which is not one of his finer efforts. One wonders whether he could have anticipated the great popularity of two short lyrics from that book, "Nothing Gold Can Stay" and "Stopping by Woods on a Snowy Evening."

Now, I intend the foregoing as my way of embarking on Paul Lindholdt's masterful first poem,

"Traveler to the Colonies," from *Making Landfall*. The 63-line poem set up in four sections or verse paragraphs initially appeared in *Sewanee Review*, as did three other poems in this collection of 46. His count in the author's note at the back appears to be a little off – not just 24, but 27 of the poems have been placed elsewhere, including such respectable journals as *Chicago Review*, *Poetry Northwest*, and *Southern Humanities Review*. The poem begins paradoxically: "It was like being forced to live / a new death with each fifth breath." In the opening section the speaker comments on the torturous ocean voyage, and here we enjoy ample evidence not only of Lindholdt's seamanship, but also of his keen ear:

Our mizzen shroud lines flapping,
the stern mast cracked and fell
across the capstan until the master
pressed a mate to hack it free.

The assonance of flapping/mast/cracked/capstan/master/hack produces a harshness appropriate to the near disaster.

In the second 16-line section, the traveler reflects on the hyperbolic promises of the "sly promoters," and here the softer [eh] assonantal cluster appears to suggest their cunning, smooth-tongued promises:

> Fish of all kinds leapt to net.
> So it seemed from what we read.
> So this place seemed
> from what the sly promoters said.

Of course, the key verb here is "seemed." But note how Lindholdt uses non-schematic rhyme in this case to effect a transition to the third section of the poem: "Instead we sleep in canvas shacks / hemmed close by ruts of mud / frozen." The word "sleep" assonantly looks (or listens) back to "seemed," and we acquire aural pairs like canvas/shacks, close/frozen, and ruts/mud. In this new world they hear "the wilderness all night / howling for our souls." Note, too, Lindholdt's confident use of line breaks: shacks-hemmed, mud-frozen, night-howling. These technical achievements indicate the work of a craftsman.

The last section of the poem opens with a rhetorical question: "How many travelers before me have you / enticed from cozy fireside to try / your surface, flattering sea?" Note the long [i], diphthong: enticed/fireside/try. The line fairly shrieks at the "sly promoters." While the other three sections of this poem run 16 lines, this one runs only 15, as if the traveler were cutting himself off in anger:

> I shall build a cedar cabin
> at Hell's Gate and rest there
> cloistered from your strumpet ways.
> I shall write the truth about this land
> and warn my countrymen to guard their eyes.

But, fanciful as this might seem, perhaps the 16th line constitutes the "truth about this land" that the traveler writes in the other poems that make up this collection.

The remaining poems of this book pick up individual accounts, many of which claim historical origins, as indicated in the half dozen pages of endnotes. The epigraph for Brooding Season, the first of the five parts into which the book is divided, is drawn from John Berryman's *Homage to Mistress Anne Bradstreet* (1956). Historical figures who make important appearances in the book include King Philip (1638-1676), the Wampanoag chief who gave his name to King Philip's War; Thomas Morton of the Maypole of Merrymount fame; Puritan minister John Cotton (grandfather of Cotton Mather); Governor John Winthrop of the Massachusetts Bay Colony and Anne Hutchinson (1591-1643) whom he banished from the colony; Increase Mather and his son Cotton, who would play a major role in the Salem witchcraft trials of 1692; Governor William Bradford of Plymouth Plantation; and Jonathan Edward, the noted sermonizer of The Great Awakening during the 1730s and '40s. Nathaniel Hawthorne would likely have appreciated these poems, but I must confess I rather missed any reference to Michael Wigglesworth and his notorious *The Day of Doom* (1662).

A few poems in this collection, while solid enough, do seem rather out of place. In the first part, "Song of Salmon," translated from Franz Boas's accounts of the Kwakiutl in the Pacific Northwest, seems to be imposed on the world Lindholdt has created here. Similarly, I'm more distracted than edified by "Tenochtitlan," which opens the third section and follows an epigraph from William Bradford. And then "Crossing Arbon Valley," a few poems later, is located on the Fort Hall Indian Reservation in southeastern Idaho, so I'm thrown off again. But when I next come upon "Moll Gone," which recalls (to me, at least) Defoe's eponymous Moll Flanders, from his 1722 novel, I do get back on track, so I'm only momentarily distracted.

The implicit question posed by my focus on the initial poem of this book is this: Do the poems live up to the promise of that first poem, that IPO? Axiomatically, I believe, not all the poems by any poet in any collection will be equally compelling. But in some ways that first poem constitutes a sort of promissory note. It offers that the poems that follow will read at least comparably well, and I think they do. The best of them are dramatic monologues, like "Famacides," "Sarah Hawkridge," "Homage to Mistress Bradford," "Rebecca Glover," "The Glare of Her Awareness," "Kit Gardiner, Banished," and particularly the paired poems, "Magistrate" and "Marianne's Quarters." These dramatic poems speak to me, often with a blending of the familiar with the exotic. We know these characters (some historic, some not) and are at least generally familiar with their circumstances, their dilemmas, but Lindholdt exposes us to some of the darkness and depravity that lurks beneath the Puritan piety. Not necessarily recommended for underage readers.

❧ Some Particulars ❦

Joan E. Bauer is author of *The Almost Sound of Drowning* (Main Street Rag, 2008). Since 2001, more than 200 of her poems have appeared in journals and anthologies in the USA and abroad. In 2007, she won the Earle Birney Poetry Prize from *Prism International*. In 2018, she was a finalist for the John Ciardi Poetry Prize from BkMk Press. For some years, she was a teacher and counselor and now divides her time between Venice, CA and Pittsburgh, PA where, along with Kristofer Collins, she co-hosts Hemingway's Summer Poetry Series.

Brenton Booth lives in Sydney, Australia.

Adam Church was raised in the DC Metro area and currently lives in Northern Virginia. He found his passion for poetry from reading Charles Bukowski and Billy Collins and the genres of folk, blues, punk and alternative music. After a hiatus from writing he is now back at the pen working on participating in the great conversation that is poetry.

Joan Colby's *Selected Poems* received the 2013 FutureCycle Prize and *Ribcage* was awarded the 2015 Kithara Book Prize. Her recent books include *Carnival* (FutureCycle) and *The Seven Heavenly Virtues* (Kelsay Books). Her latest book is *Her Heartstrings* (Presa, 2018).

Sandy Coomer is an artist, Ironman athlete, and social entrepreneur in Nashville, TN. Her poetry has been published in numerous journals and she is author of three poetry chapbooks and a full-length collection, *Available Light* (Iris Press). More than 150 pieces of Sandy's art have been published in literary arts magazines. Sandy is a poetry mentor in the AWP Writer to Writer Mentorship Program and founding editor of *Rockvale Review*. She is founder and director of Rockvale Writers' Colony in College Grove, TN, a not-for-profit organization that exists to support, promote, and educate writers of all genres and backgrounds.

Rachel Custer is author of *The Temple She Became* (Five Oaks, 2017). Her work is constantly informed by and wrestles with the values and struggles of the rural Rust Belt. Her Christian faith is vital to her understanding of the world and her art. She lives with her partner and their daughter in Northern Indiana. She has previously published poetry, personal essays, and flash fiction in many literary journals such as *Rattle*,

The American Journal of Poetry B O D Y, (PANK), DIALOGIST, and *The Journal of Applied Poetics.*

Michael Czyzniejewski is author of three collections of short stories, most recently *I Will Love You for the Rest of My Life: Breakup Stories* (Curbside Splendor, 2015). He serves as literary editor of Moon City Press and editor-in-chief of *Moon City Review*. In 2009, he was awarded a National Endowment for the Arts fellowship in prose.

Sarah Daugherty has an MFA in creative writing from Cal State: Long Beach. Her poetry and short fiction has appeared in *November 3rd Club, Pearl, Bicycle Review, Poets Against War.*

W.D. Ehrhart's most recent book is *Thank you For Your Service: Collected Poems* (McFarland, 2019).

Edward Field's first publication was in 1949, a poem in *Poetry Quarterly* (London). Since then he's published several books of poetry, a translation of Inuit poems, a travel diary about Afghanistan, novels written with his blind partner Neil Derrick, a memoir of his colorful friends, and edited two anthologies.

Marja Hagborg lives and writes in Chicago with her Viking husband and two cats.

Ruth Moon Kempher is publisher of King Estate Press, St. Augustine, FL. She's retired from teaching and tavern owning and now concentrates on travel, writing and caring for her housemate, a chocolate lab named Miss Brie. Her latest books are *In Magickal Waters* (Finishing Line, 2017), *The Skinny About J.'s Zinnias – & Other Night Notes* (Chiron Review, 2016), and *What I Can Tell You* (Bright Hill, 2013).

Kyle Laws is based out of the Arts Alliance Studios in Pueblo, CO where she directs Line/Circle: Women Poets in Performance. Her collections include *Ride the Pink Horse* (Stubborn Mule), *Faces of Fishing Creek* (Middle Creek), *So Bright to Blind* (Five Oaks), and *Wildwood* (Lummox). Her poems and essays have appeared in magazines and anthologies in the US, UK, Canada, France, and Germany.

Lyn Lifshin (1942-2019): For her absolute dedication to the small presses which first published her, and for managing to survive on her own apart from any major publishing house or academic institution, Lyn earned the distinction, "Queen of the Small Presses." She was praised by Robert Frost, Ken Kesey, and Richard Eberhart. Ed Sanders has described her as "a modern Emily Dickinson." She was winner of numerous awards including the Jack Kerouac Award for her book *Kiss The Skin Off*, and subject of the documentary film *Lyn Lifshin: Not Made of Glass*.

klipschutz' latest collection is *Premeditations* (2019, Hoot n Waddle). He lives in San Francisco with Colette Jappy, and three tuxedo cats.

Ron McFarland lives in Moscow, ID, where he has dwelt nigh onto 50 years. Since retiring from U of Idaho English department in 2018, he has continued to write poems and prose. His current project is a book-length study of hyper-prolific Chicano writer Gary Soto.

Tamara Madison is author of the chapbook *The Belly Remembers*, and two volumes of poetry, *Wild Domestic* and *Moraine* (all Pearl Editions). Her work has appeared in *Your Daily Poem, A Year of Being Here, Nerve Cowboy, Writer's Almanac, Sheila-Na-Gig,* and many other publications.

DS Maolalai is a graduate of English literature from Trinity College in Dublin, lives in Toronto, is author of *Love is Breaking Plates in the Garden* (Encircle Publ.), and has appeared in such places as *4'33', Strange Bounce and Bong is Bard, Down in the Dirt Magazine, Out of Ours, Eunoia Review, Kerouac's Dog, More Said Than Done, Star Tips, Myths Magazine, Ariadne's Thread, Belleville Park Pages, Killing the Angel,* and *Unrorean Broadsheet*.

Alicia Mathias is a poet, photographer, and singer. Her poems have recently appeared in: *Ann Arbor Review, The Bitter Oleander, The Canopy Review, Clockwise Cat, January Review Journal, Unlikely Stories Mark V,* and elsewhere. She lives and writes in New York, with her favorite muse, Zeppelin the Wonder Cat.

Fox Mederos is a Cuban American first-generation writer. He has a bachelor's degree in creative writing from California State U, Long

Beach, where he was also awarded the Beatrice and John Janosco scholarship prize for his poetry. He lives in Culver City, CA where he takes care of his grandmother. "Goat Story" is his first publication.

Roger Netzer's poems have appeared in *Green Hills Literary Lantern, The Potomac*, and *Chiron Review*.

Chika Onyenezi is a fiction candidate at Maryland U's MFA. Born in Owerri, Nigeria, his work has appeared, or is forthcoming in *Scoundrel Time, American InItalia, Chicago Quarterly Review, Cosmonauts Avenue, Apogee, Ninth Letter, Evergreen Review*, and elsewhere. He is a 2018 Kimbilio Fellow, and a 2019 writer-in-residence at Craigarden.

Jonah Raskin is a northern California performance poet and author of *American Scream: Allen Ginsberg's 'Howl' and the Making of the Beat Generation*.

James Reed's fiction has appeared in such journals as *Juked, Dogwood, River Styx*, and *The Gettysburg Review*, and among other honors he holds a Fellowship from the National Endowment for the Arts.

Diane Sahms, a native Philadelphian poet, has four collections of her poetry published, most recently *The Handheld Mirror of the Mind* (*Kelsay Books*, 2018). Diane's poems have been widely published in the small and electronic press. Poetry editor of *North of Oxford*, she works full-time for the federal government as a buyer.

Steve Sibra grew up in a very small farming town in eastern Montana. For 35 years, he has made his living by buying and selling vintage comic books. Steve's writing has appeared in *Matador Review, Jersey Devil Press, Gravel* and elsewhere. He has work forthcoming in the gun-violence anthology, *Humans in the Wild*.

Kareem Tayyar's novel *The Prince of Orange County* (Pelekinesis, 2018), was a finalist for an Independent Book Award, and his poetry and fiction has been published in a variety of journals, including *Alaska Quarterly Review, Brilliant Corners, The Santa Monica Review*, and *The Writer's Almanac*. He holds a PhD in English from UC Riverside, and he is a recipient of a 2019 Wurlitzer Poetry Fellowship.

David J. Thompson is a former prep school teacher and coach who lives in Chapel Hill, NC. His interests include movies, *The Simpsons*, and minor league baseball. His latest poetry/photography book is *Grace Takes Me* (Vegetarian Alcoholic Press). A series of 1,400 of his postcards is now part of the permanent collection at Newberry Library in Chicago. Please visit his photo website at ninemilephoto.com.

Jeri Thompson is a poet living in Long Beach, CA, and has her degree from CSULB. Nominated for a Pushcart Prize in 2014, she is in numerous publications, her proudest; *Chiron Review*. Also, *The Fox Poetry Box, Carnival Lit Magazine*, Silver Birch Press (*Silver, Green, and Summer*), *Red Light Lit*, and *Anti Heroin Chic*.

Charles Harper Webb's latest book, *What Things Are Made Of*, was published by the U of Pittsburgh in 2013. *Brain Camp* was published by Pitt in 2015. Recipient of grants from the Whiting and Guggenheim foundations, Webb teaches in the MFA Program in Creative Writing at California State University, Long Beach.

John Sibley Williams is author of *As One Fire Consumes Another* (Orison Poetry Prize, 2019), *Skin Memory* (Backwaters Prize, U of Nebraska, 2019), *Summon* (JuxtaProse Chapbook Prize, 2019), *Disinheritance*, and *Controlled Hallucinations*. A 22-time Pushcart nominee, John is winner of numerous awards, including Wabash Prize for Poetry, Philip Booth Award, *American Literary Review* Poetry Contest, Laux/Millar Prize, Phyllis Smart-Young Prize, Janet B. McCabe Poetry Prize, and others. He serves as editor of *The Inflectionist Review,* and works as a poetry editor and literary agent. Previous publishing credits include: *The Yale Review, North American Review, Midwest Quarterly, Southern Review, Sycamore Review, Prairie Schooner, Massachusetts Review, Poet Lore, Saranac Review, Atlanta Review, TriQuarterly, Columbia Poetry Review, Mid-American Review, Poetry Northwest, Third Coast*, and various anthologies. He lives in Portland, OR.

Kristin Withers resides in the Pacific Northwest. She has been an industrial sewist, coffee roaster, bookseller, realty & teaching assistant. Kristin is currently working on several concept collections.

❧ *Our Patrons* ❦

Brenton Booth
Blue Horse Press
Alan Catlin
W.D. Ehrhart
Favorite Sister
Roman Gladstone
David & Vicki Greisman
Robert Headley
John Jacob
Max Mavis
Shawn Pavey
Reckless
Glenn Sheldon
Jared Smith
Marc Swan
Thespis & Minou
Ralph F. Voss

(27) Anonymous

❧ *Special Thanks* ❦

Gerald Locklin
Putzina Press